I <u>am</u> grateful for your
kindness, Robert.
May all of your days be
filled with love and wonder —

Marcelle Martyn

New Ages and Other Wonders

Marcella Martyn

BALBOA.
PRESS

A DIVISION OF HAY HOUSE

Balboa Press books may be ordered through booksellers or by contacting:

Balboa Press
A Division of Hay House
1663 Liberty Drive
Bloomington, IN 47403
www.balboapress.com
1-(877) 407-4847

Printed in the United States of America

ISBN: 978-1-4525-6601-6 (sc)
ISBN: 978-1-4525-6603-0 (hc)
ISBN: 978-1-4525-6602-3 (e)

Library of Congress Control Number: 2012924007

Balboa Press rev. date: 12/28/2012

Also by Marcella Martyn:

I AM HERE, Channeled Wisdom for Changing Times.
Balboa Press, 2011

To the survivors and the seekers, who chose the rockiest paths on their journeys. They survived abuse, neglect, pain, poverty, illness, and loss and still found the strength to empower and enlarge their souls beyond expectation. During the darkest nights of their souls, they remembered their light and sought the divine. Rising from the ashes, they found their wings. They learned to chase love in the shadows and to give to others what they had not received. I hold them in the highest esteem and pray that love and peace accompany them along their way.

Contents

Chapter One

ASCENSION/HOME

I am here. It is good to speak with you again so soon. I am pleased that you are ready to begin again. There is much still to discuss.

Let us talk more of the changes being made manifest upon the earth plane. Please remember that the influence of that third dimensional plane extends outside of the solar system of which the sun, planets, and moons are a part. It was necessary at the creation of the earthen physical plane to extend the physicality beyond the solar system because all that could be seen and known from the earth was integral to the workings of the physical energy grids. The earth system was designed both to house and to hide the illusions created.

Each part of the system plays its part in the maintenance of the manifestation of energy as matter. It is a very intricate energy system employing the energies contained in each of the planetary and star bodies, just as each human, animal, or plant body is maintained through the interaction of all of its cells and organs. So it is with the physical plane. Each movement, each ray of energy or light, each position affects the operation of the whole. While it is a complex organization, it is not a static organization. It too carries life or it could not exist. Like all living physical systems, it also is in a constant state of growth and change, with each part interconnected and cooperative toward the same goal.

As change occurs in any part of the unified system, adjustments are then made within all of the other components. This is how those with the knowledge of the workings of the earth and the heavens could read the changes taking place, by watching for the visible changes in the individual patterns, locations, and movements of the celestial bodies in times past.

These memories of the true nature of the suns, planets, and moons shall be returned to mankind with the return of the light. And so shall the knowledge of the living nature of all be remembered. As a result, the honor and respect due to the earth system shall once again be restored. The life essences of the material in all of its many forms shall be also remembered as the unity of all life is again restored. Let us speak further of this next time. I am your friend and servant.

Rashka, September 30, 2011

I am here. I am your friend Rashka. It is wonderful to be speaking with you again. Let us begin.

We spoke last of the upcoming changes to that physical plane. Among the changes soon to be in evidence in that plane will be the overlaying of a unity grid. So much that was necessary for the return of heaven to earth has already been established that it is now the next logical step in that place. The knowledge of the unity of all beings will be essential to the implementation and utilization of the energy changes already placed within the mechanics of the new earth.

As we have discussed at an earlier time, the very nature of the physics of the material plane will be changed from the old system of cause and effect to a new, purer system of cooperation that is much more in alignment with the workings of universal law. It follows, therefore, that the cooperative, connected nature of all things both material and energetic is a key element in the proper workings of the new earth.

As you are aware, under the physical laws of the old earth change in the forms of energy and matter had been affected, for the most part, by the exertion of energy upon a material substance toward a designed goal of converting the status of the material or releasing energy from the material. This system was, at best, artificial and at its worst was contrary to the natural universal law of energy and matter. Outside of the physical planes all such alteration of the manifest form of energy is accomplished by consensus or cooperation.

It shall soon again be so in that plane. I am sure that you can understand that this system requiring cooperation and consent is fully reliant upon the concept of recognition of the consciousness of all energy and matter. It is the remembrance of consciousness of being that shall first be exposed by the unity grid. It shall then be easier to return the knowledge of the interconnected nature of all of life. It then follows that the cooperative ventures between the energetic and material kingdoms can again be implemented. Through the use of this old system, that we are referring to as new, all that is needed or desired will be made manifest without the use of force once again. It is inherent within this system that no thing that does not serve the best interests of all can be made manifest within the physical plane. The consent required to create any thing that serves less than the whole will not be achieved.

Please consider that the ideal state of being under universal law includes happiness, abundance, and fulfillment of purpose, and, therefore, the achievement of these goals for a part of the whole of mankind or any other physical element or kingdom is in the best interest of the whole. The destruction or exclusion of any part of the whole is not in alignment with universal law and consent for a goal of these types will not be given. That is as it should be.

In the ancient times this was understood and, therefore, permission was always asked of any material being from which a change in form or location was desired. Permission asked and granted was always preferable to forgiveness asked and granted. This change in the operation of all matter and energy within the physical is substantial. I am sure you can understand why the remembrance of this concept is critical to the proper functioning of the new energies that are already in place but as yet unseen and not yet empowered.

Let us speak again soon. Until then, my friend, stay in the light and remember who you are.

Rashka, October 9, 2011

I am here. I am your friend Rashka. I am glad to be speaking with you again. We have much to discuss. May we begin?

Upon the new earth there shall be much of what exists in the higher dimensions that has not been present in that place for very long periods of time. Although it shall, at first glance, seem very unfamiliar, when it is examined by the heart and soul there shall be remembrances brought forth of other planes and experiences that shall very quickly alleviate any anxiety surrounding these new conditions. I know that you have asked about the return of heaven to earth and wondered "what then"? I wish to answer your concerns, as they are based in a human context and even though all souls of the earth shall be ascended and enlightened, they shall still be ascended and enlightened humans.

Although such a type of human has not existed before, they shall still be gifted with the circumstances of heaven and the universal laws while retaining much that is human. They will then experience periods of adjustment to their changed circumstances that shall, of course, vary between individuals, even though they shall also be unified and reconnected to the truth of their beings. In and upon the new earth, all shall be possible and the miraculous shall become the rule, rather than the exception.

Humans worry so about making mistakes. It is entertaining, but pointless. When the energies of heaven return to the earth, all shall see all others in their truth and beauty. All shall see All That Is in its truth and beauty. Under these circumstances of unity and awareness, it shall not be possible to create a mistake or perform a misdeed. When operating from within a mindful or ego based thought process, it is possible to adversely affect another being, although these acts and thoughts have always been only transitory in nature, but when operating from a heart based system the same shall not be possible or even desired. Any interaction between beings shall be cooperative and fully aware. Can you understand how it would not be possible to manipulate or abuse any being while fully aware of their true essence and the interconnected nature of all to each other?

Mistakes and misdeeds are of the old earth and, as such, only occurred out of blindness. All that exists, or will exist, within the energies of the new earth shall be of love. By its very nature, nothing that would do harm can exist in love. However, in an existence based in and created from love, anything that can be imagined can be created, through cooperation of all of the interconnected elements of the dream. Humans and the other elements of earth and the heavens shall find and share great joy in creation, uncreation, and recreation, as it pleases them. It shall seem to be new territory, but only for a very short period of time, after which it will seem as though this state of being and creating is all that ever was upon the earth.

And so, my friend, the answer to your original question of "what then" is … anything that your hearts desire. That is the way of the universe and so it shall also be the way of the earth.

Rashka, February 18, 2012

I am here. I am glad to be in your presence once again. I am called by the name of Isahal and I am a teacher of the ways of the universe. I come this day to teach and also to learn. I am grateful for this opportunity to speak with you again. You have much on your mind and I am happy to be of assistance to you.

There is much change afoot on that physical plane at this time. I know that you feel the energy changes, as do all upon the planet, at this time. I ask that you be as gentle toward yourself as you are with others. This time, and the times that follow so closely, will be trying, as the necessary adjustments are being made within the physical to accommodate the increasing light energies of the spiritual. Thoughts of peace and acceptance of these changes as a natural course shall bring some ease to the physical and emotional turmoil.

An old age passes away now, as a new age dawns. Remember at all times, if you can, a correlation to the process of birth. Remember the physical changes that led to the entrance into life of a new human upon the earth. Remember how quickly the pain and turmoil passes into joy larger than could have been imagined with the birth of a new child. So goes now the process upon, within, and among the planet and all who call her home. All is as it should be and the reward is mightier than can be seen from within the process.

Please remember that all who cross into this new age chose their participation in this momentous event. There is great honor and greater courage involved in this choice, for when the choice to participate was made the outcome of this adventure was not yet fully formed and complete in its design. Many chose to attempt this ascension merely out of faith and hope, and with no certainty of success. Now it has come to pass that the hopes and dreams brought to that plane have surpassed expectations.

This time upon the earth is like no other in her glorious past, and the energies and souls of the universe are very elated to also be able to participate in this ascension process. Just as many souls chose to incarnate during these times of change, so also did many of the ascended souls and guardians also choose to stand by the planet and her children at this time. They serve and await service with the same faith and hope that inspired the dream from its inception. And so it is that for many years of your time there have been present within your universe a multitude of observers, guides, and masters supporting the progression of humankind toward this very time.

As you know, as the energies of the new earth establish themselves within that realm, many who have served in silence and disguised their presence shall be released and can show themselves in their truth and service. This time approaches rapidly and is cause for celebration among those who wait and those who serve. They have patiently waited for the time when they can be joined once again with the earth and the children of light within and upon the earth. I stand among these souls and also yearn for the reconnections that the lifting of the veil will allow. We are aware that when the servants of the earth are once again revealed in their light bodies, many who have slumbered or forgotten themselves shall remember what they truly are. We are filled with joy at this prospect.

Outside of the constraints of time, we know that this time of awakening and communion is now fixed within the plan and the process. I understand that within the constraints of time it will feel as though promises of ascension are not being kept, but that is untrue. We are but a breath and a step away. Your hope and faith have created a miracle. Hold tight to them for but a while longer.

Isahal, March 14, 2012

I am here. I am your teacher Josiah. It has been too long since we have spoken. I am pleased to be with you once again. If I may, I would like to begin the discussion of our next topic.

Let us speak of heaven. Each man's soul holds a remembrance of heaven, which I would prefer to call home for the purposes of our discussion, if you have no objection. Thank you. While incarnate in a physical dimension, or for that matter in another dimension operating in a limited state, very little memory of home is accessible. I am certain that you understand the purpose of this. At any time all souls are welcome at home. Those who choose to send a part of themselves into a limited dimension often choose these planes of existence to experience situations and relationships that are without the unity and love which is omnipresent at home. A series of lessons or experiences are designed within these incarnate lifetimes that express a set or series of desired learning experiences for, with, and in opposition to parts of other souls, who also choose these experiences. It is not at all necessary that these incarnate lives contain, express, or resolve difficulties or conflicts. It is most often the case that these are the exact circumstances chosen, particularly within the physical dimensions, because these types of experiences contain the highest potential for rapid soul growth.

It is precisely because of these types of conflicts and difficulties that memories of home are left behind when souls make these life plans and choices. A memory of home and the remembrance of the joy of returning home would provide a disincentive to follow the course of learning.

In what may seem to be direct opposition to my previous statement, it is, however, often the case that when a life plan is chosen that contains a very high level of difficulty, an incarnating soul can retain memories of home. These memories are generally enclosed inside of extrasensory gifts or are implanted into the life course as experiences that awaken these memories, as a tool to prevent damage to the soul that would necessitate substantial healing because of the wounds acquired in an overly ambitious life course.

Limited access to memories of home is the general rule. Fuller access is the exception to the rule. This has been the way of the old earth. It will remain, in a diminished form, in the new earth. During the transition between the two, much awakening of these memories of home will transpire for a great number of incarnate souls, as the increased level of awakening aids the process of transformation of the physical planes.

Although the new state of the physical planes will allow them to function with more aspects of home in their design, they will not be identical to home. There would be no reason for their existence if they were too similar to home. Do you understand my point?

When it is stated that the new time of the earth returns heaven to earth, it does not mean that heaven overlays earth fully. Earth and the counterparts of a physical nature will continue to exist in form, as its form fits its function and purpose. The change arriving, even as we speak, is monumental and unprecedented. The change will heighten access to heaven from earth and will heighten access to the earth from heaven.

Much, but not all, that was hidden will be revealed. In doing so, heaven allows the functionality of the physical planes to align with the ways of home. Please take notice of my words. I said that access to the ways of home will be allowed. I did not say that they would be demanded.

The purpose and function of the physical planes is to provide a platform for experiencing and evolving of souls. In the new earth, this will allow for the lessons and evolution of souls that are awake to the ways of home to create new and exciting types of life plans and experiences in closer alignment with the universal laws of unity and love. It will be the choice of each soul whether they desire to experience these planes awakened.

Much that exists within these physical planes has remained hidden during the life of the old earth. In the life of the new earth, much that has been hidden will be revealed. Much more that has been hidden will be accessible. These changes will allow for a fuller, more connected experience within these planes. The choice remains, still, with the incarnating souls to access or ignore the increased presence of home. This is as it should be.

Josiah the Teacher, October 12, 2012

I am here. I am your friend and guide. I am happy to be with you and I would also like to share my information about home.

At home all souls exist within the love and the light of All That Is. All that can be imagined or dreamed is possible; therefore, home can be experienced in many ways. There is no single correct vision of heaven, as it is all things to all beings.

In a whole, unified state of being, it is experienced as light that is pure, white, and brighter than you can imagine. It also is constructed, imbued, and formed by the purest of unconditional love. This is the state of home that welcomes returning souls. It is in this state of love and light that souls rejoin their soul groups and heal and realign with the parts of their own wholeness that were not carried into a dimension designed for incarnations. This pure state of home is literally the light at the end of the tunnel that is sought by souls in transition out of an incarnation. Even a frightened or damaged soul will recognize this purity and be drawn by its presence.

Once a returning soul is rejoined with the light of home, the variations of the next moment are infinite. Each returning soul carries, from the journey just undertaken, memories of the experience that influence its experience of heaven. All due care is taken to ease the return and readjustment of each soul, so it is often the case that a soul's expectation of the experience creates it. This is in no way indicative of punishment or judgment imposed from outside of a soul's own wishes. The process of readjustment does, however, involve merging the experiences of the lifetime into the greater essence of the soul. It is often most easily done within a framework of a created space and situation that serves as a transition between the dimension that was left and the dimension entered, which often holds components and properties of both. This created space is temporary and is constructed for only as long as needed to accomplish the readjustment. Although these conditions are actually created by the returning soul, guidance and assistance is always given during this realignment by others.

Souls who return from darker dimensions or who have returned home under emotionally charged circumstances are capable of creating very dark spaces in which to begin the transition to wholeness. It is these dark place memories that are the foundation of the myths of hell, purgatory, and the like in human cultures. Please know that any such creation is only a reaction to an individual soul's expectation, and is not real. Each returning soul is lovingly and carefully guided and protected through their transition and is in a constant state of movement toward realignment with the truth of its unified essence.

Home is composed of love. Home does not judge or punish. It only loves. Because the experiences of each returning soul are different, each soul's process of readjusting to home is also different to some degree. All are protected and healed. All are loved.

Let us speak of this again, as there is much that I would like to tell you about home. It just felt right to start at the beginning today.

Serrale, October 16, 2012

I am here. I am your teacher Isahal. I have come into your presence this day to discuss heaven. May we begin?

The workings of heaven are much less complex than the workings of the physical dimensions and it is this simplicity that gives home its glory. Heaven is not a place. Heaven is a state of being that operates under the universal laws of love and unity. All that is created is formed from energy and the energy is love expressed in its simplest state. All that exist are unified. All are one. Simple. At home all beings know that they are one being. At home all beings know love.

Security in the knowledge that each being is an integral part of a whole being is what makes home heaven. All that any being wishes to experience or learn is available to them, for they contain the essence of a creator. What one is, all are. What one creates, all create. What one knows, all know. Harm or mischief directed to another is foreign to heaven, simply because there is no difference between the self and the all.

All that was ever created exists in the present moment. All that will be created in the future exists in the present moment. Any arrangement of creations or events into sequences of events or separate creations is only a choice exercised by a part, or cooperative parts, of the one for a chosen purpose. These choices are the basis of all other dimensions, times, and events outside of heaven. I understand that may seem confusing, but I will try to explain.

The created universes are not truly outside of heaven, but in order for anything to exist in a state that is not whole, it cannot operate or exist within wholeness. The existence outside of the unified state of All That Is necessitates the creation of a barrier, of sorts, between the home and the other, or the other will operate as home. I think that you understand, but I will give a simple example. When in darkness, the darkness exists without the benefit of light. It seems to be separate or removed from the light. When light enters the darkness, it is darkness no more. It is then light. In truth, it always was light, but light withheld itself from the place that darkness chose to exhibit itself as a part of the light, rather than the wholeness of the light. It is so with heaven. When heaven envelops the place that a non-heaven space has been created; that space returns to its fullness of being as heaven.

Within heaven all beings are free to express themselves as a part of their wholeness. The difference, however, between this expression of less than wholeness and the expression of separation is significant. In heaven, a soul can choose to expand, learn, teach, or experience for itself, but each always carries the knowledge of unity, whether or not it chooses to express its being as separate. Please understand that each soul does not believe that it is unified with the whole. Each soul does not think that it is unified with the whole. Each being knows that it is unified with the whole. This knowingness is a part of its essence.

This will be a good place to stop.

Isahal, October 18, 2012

I am here. I am your teacher Isahal. I am glad to be with you once again. May we continue our discussion of home?

When at home, all souls continue to learn as well as teach. Because it feels familiar to earth souls, we gather in magnificent halls of learning and share information and experiences. Many souls do not incarnate as humans and are anxious to learn of the experiences of those souls who choose physical incarnations. Many souls who are between incarnations also choose to study at home. Teaching and learning are quite different than that conducted in the earth schools, however. Information shared in the schools of home is complete. Students do not research and listen to lectures. Information shared in this manner is always limited and incomplete. Instead, the student joins with the energetic essence of the subject, under the guidance of the teachers, and in this the whole of a piece of knowledge or an experience can be shared. Please remember that only the present moment exists at home and the knowledge shared is experienced in this state. All That Is changes constantly and so, also, does all knowledge and experience. For this reason, no course of study is truly finite or complete. Learning is an ever continuing process because the material being studied is in a constant state of change.

At home, all souls engage themselves in any manner that suits their development, their curiosity, or their creativity, all the while serving the whole of creation. Some teach, some guide, some service the elements of the created universes. Some collect and hold knowledge. Some disperse knowledge. Some create music, art, and beauty. All serve out of love for their service. All are respected and honored, not only for their service, but also for their inherent beauty and value. All are a beloved aspect of All That Is. Each does what he loves and each is loved unconditionally at each and every moment. It can be no other way. Love is the essence of home and it is love that binds all of life together.

You are correct that being loved is the ultimate freedom. At home, all souls are known to be perfect parts of a perfect whole. All that love can create can be created by any being operating from within love. Each is as powerful and wise as the whole. All are as one. This is the true and natural state of all beings at home. We have told you before that home is not a place, but is rather a state of being. This is true. When any soul touches this state of being, it touches home. Home is not a place. Home is not a concept. Home is not a destination. Home is a unified state of being with all of creation and All That Is. That state of being feels like love, acceptance, peace, and joy. It feels like home.

Isahal, November 1, 2012

Chapter Two

PRE-BIRTH PLANNING

I am here. I am your friend Rashka and I am so glad that you asked to speak with me this day. I will be very glad to answer your question. May we begin?

Before entering into a lifetime in the earth plane, or any of the other physical planes, a great deal of planning takes place. Each soul that is considering such a lifetime generally has decided that there is either unfinished business from a previous incarnation or has found an area of interest that it wishes to explore further through a physical experience. I say that this is generally the case, as there are exceptions that we will discuss further.

After the idea of an incarnation has formed, the members of a soul's group of advisors and companions approach the soul to share the idea. I am sorry. This is difficult to explain because of the nature of communication outside of the physical plane. Perhaps we should discuss this now, to be sure that you can better understand this process. All thought and experience exists in its own right and carries its own light and life force, both within and outside of the physical planes. This is one of the forms of energy and life that are veiled in the physical universes.

Although there are many souls who carry a knowledge of this into a physical lifetime, only a relative few also carry the keys, if you will, to this information. These keys are called by many names on the earth; such as ESP, prophesy, divine revelation, witchery, and insanity, among other names. To those who can access this living information and experience, it appears as a reality or a truth. To those who do not remember the living forms of experience and thought, it is generally treated with disdain or fear. Among the non-human kingdoms of the earth, this fact is remembered almost universally and is utilized, in addition to or in place of language, for communication purposes. There is a concept of its use among animals, in particular, as access to a collective consciousness; however, this concept is, as much within the physical planes, only part of the truth of the matter.

In the nonphysical universe, thought and experience are living, conscious, forms of energy able to call unto themselves other beings or consciousness with whom they wish to share themselves. It is this way with the formation of a thought of incarnation. Upon completion of the formation of the idea, it is the idea, or plan itself, that shares itself with all who find an interest in the matter. Because time and space are only created dimensions within physical universes, they do not factor into the process, therefore, there are no aspects of this process related to meetings or schedules as they are known on your plane. This gathering, for lack of a better term, happens instantaneously as there is no other way within universal law.

As we have discussed in the past, the ways of the universe are simple and are, thus, often difficult to frame within a human reference of complexity. I do not digress from your question for any reason other than clarity, and feel that an explanation of this communication form will prove to be relevant to the topic at hand. All That Is is constantly connected to and in communication with all of its aspects and components All that is known or experienced by any aspect of the All, which includes any one or any thing that exists in any form or any place, is knowable to any and all parts of itself. All that exists in any form or any place, as an aspect or component of All That Is, lives, therefore, communication and sharing of information, experience, or emotion is a living thing rather than a process, in truth, but for ease of communication between you and I, it shall be referred to as a process because that is easier to understand from your earthly point of view.

Please let that settle in for a while and we will continue this discussion again very soon.

Rashka, March 18, 2012

I am here. I am your friend Rashka and I am glad to be with you once again. I will be happy to continue our previous discussion of the planning process, as I promised. There is much understanding to be gained from this information that may prove to be of much comfort to you and to others. It is my pleasure to serve your curiosity on this subject and I am aware that you will be sharing this information also, which makes our discussion of this topic all the more important.

Let us begin again. As we discussed before, a soul decides to incarnate in a physical lifetime and this idea or plan then goes forth to share of itself with other souls who share this common interest. As you know, while in a physical plane each participant in, or observer of, any experience knows, feels, or sees only part of the truth of the experience because of the physical and energetic limitations inherent in a physical dimension. Outside of the physical planes, however, the same experience exists in a more complete, more whole, state of being.

So it is with the experiences being planned before each incarnation. Much like staging a theatrical production, the planning process represents the writing of the script, staging the sets, and choosing the cast. In execution of the physical experience, the script is often subject to revision as the production progresses, even while the basic core idea remains intact.

Inside of this analogy, participation of the players, musicians, stage hands, and prospective audience members are determined pre-production, but are also subject to change as the production approaches. The soul who designed the idea or plan serves as the director and producer of the play, and the members of the cast choose their roles for reasons of their own. Some choose to participate because they seek the challenge of the role. Some choose to participate in order to expand upon a previous role within the same genre. Some choose to play a hero, while some choose to play a villain. Some choose a major role, whilst others choose a bit part. Some choose to work unseen behind the scenes. Some choose a seat in the audience, in preparation for a role in another production at a later date, while others choose to observe as a comparison of a previous portrayal with the current players. Some choose to participate out of respect for the director/play writer only, but ultimately each chooses his own place in the planned production of his own free will. Whether participating to be of service or to gain from the experience in some way, each chooses his part in the play.

Some of the participants are beloved members of the same group of souls who often incarnate together. Others serve different soul groups, but choose to experience the plan as an individual during the planned lifetime and will share the experience with their soul group upon their return home.

Each and all souls participating in the experiences of the planned incarnation serve in love. I know that this can seem hard to understand, but it is true. Please remember that the experiences of a lifetime are temporal, while the life of a soul is eternal. Please remember that all who play a part in any experience within a physical lifetime choose their own part in the experiences to learn, to teach, or both at the same time. And so the process is repeated for each experience that a soul chooses to experience within an incarnation. An experience or lesson is chosen, each and another choose to aid in manifesting the experience for itself and for another, or many others, until all roles are cast.

Please be assured that all planning is gently monitored and guided by those souls who guide and protect each soul involved in the process. Much advice and support is available to each soul as they all make their choices, and during and after each chosen experience, to assure that no harm befalls any of the players. Please also know that guidance and protection also allow and contribute to changes of the circumstances and roles of the participants as the life experiences progress, again for the protection of the players.

Outside of a physical dimension all things are loving and simple. It is understood that any lifetime in a physical dimension is but a fleeting moment in the life of a soul. Much guidance is given to lighten the burdens and harshness of the planned experiences. In many of the physical dimensions the planning is quite fixed and exacting to assure that the lifetime, or lifetimes, does not over tax the souls. In these cases much less experiencing of a difficult nature is allowed, and growth and learning progress much more gently and at a much slower rate. This is good, and lifetimes are much kinder and much more managed and guided.

The earth plane is the exception, rather than the rule, as most physical planes do not allow for free will within an incarnation. This is why only the bravest of souls choose the earth plane. There is much faster evolution among souls in the earth plane, but it also carries a much greater risk to the souls involved. No harm to any soul is ever permanent; all damage will be healed, but there are easier means to evolution of souls than your planet of free choice. We will discuss how these risks are managed and mitigated at a later time. For now, I am your friend and servant.

Rashka, March 23, 2012

I am here. I am your friend Rashka. I am happy to be in your presence once again. Let us continue our previous topic, if we may.

It is an essential element of the pre-birth planning of a soul that cooperation be achieved between all parties to the lessons and experiences of an incarnation. As a part of this cooperative situation, it is often the fact that agreements are reached between souls to serve and be served during the lifetime. Each incarnating soul will generally desire as broad and full an experience as possible within such a short time as is provided by a human lifetime. Whenever two or more of any forms of energy interact, there are exchanges of energy or knowledge between or among them. During the design of the plan of a lifetime, every effort is made to assure that the needs and desires of all souls involved will be met during the exchanges and experiences so planned.

I am discussing this element of the planning process in an attempt to inform about the nature of interactions between souls on the earth plane, which directly affects the duration and intensity of the experiences shared by the souls. When the planned experiences are representative of significant matters of healing or evolution, it is often the case that many exchanges between or among the souls will be required to achieve the desired result. It is generally quite a complex arrangement or agreement when all parties to the lesson are involved in significant lessons. Because of the necessity for interactions and exchanges that require resolution within the planned lifetime, or that require balancing of energy or power exchanges between the souls, these are either relationships of long duration or great intensity.

In these cases, the commitments created between the souls are great and these experiences are most often shared between souls who share a great commitment to each other prior to the planned lifetime. Human interactions that will be of long duration, by earth standards, or are of high intensity, require a strong underlying current of love, respect, and trust. So it is that those souls who choose to share the most complex or most traumatic experiences during a lifetime are those who also share the strongest connections outside of their incarnations. These agreements between and among beloved souls are easily reached when the desired lesson is loving, balancing, or educational in nature and derive their need of commitment only from the duration of the exchanges required to complete the cycle of the lesson or lessons. These agreements are also more easily reached when the lesson or lessons involve a process that is mutually beneficial to all souls involved in relatively equal measure. For example, should one soul desire to experience the lesson of learning to love another who exhibits one or more traits that the soul could judge as abhorrent, this lesson is best fulfilled with a soul who wishes to learn that all beings deserve to be loved without judgment. Although this lesson may require a commitment to a great deal of time, relative to the duration of this lifetime, both souls will be serving each other in a state of relative balance and both stand to benefit in the same measure. Do you understand? Good.

Agreements are also often easily reached when the lesson is one of great intensity, but the duration of the experience is relatively short, allowing both or all souls to move quickly to their next lesson or to return home quickly after the energy exchange is made. When the desired lesson can be accomplished within a quick, intense burst, particularly when the experience involves great trauma or loss or if the lesson does not involve a complete resolution for all souls involved, these exchanges also require a strong commitment between the souls, but only for a very short time. When the planned intense experience is, for the most part, mutually beneficial to all souls involved, the agreement is generally easily reached. When these intense or long term lessons are not mutually beneficial, that is another matter altogether.

The creation of a situation wherein imbalance or potential trauma exists within the plan is arranged between, and performed by, the most loving and connected souls. Although that may not, at first glance, seem logical, it is very true. Most often, the most difficult lessons can only be shared out of the most love. Love and respect are the way of All That Is. Denial of these attributes, in any form, to another soul is the most difficult choice that a soul can make, and participation in such an endeavor is an act of true love and sacrifice for another.

As we discussed previously, a series of agreements are made by and between souls prior to an incarnation in an earth life. The lengths and levels of emotion and commitment within these exchanges vary quite widely, dependent upon the lesson and the service being provided by the souls involved. As we have previously discussed the situations that require the most commitment, I would now like to discuss the nature and misunderstood importance of the energy exchanges at the other end of the spectrum; being those that are brief or small energy exchanges between souls. I call these misunderstood because the duration and intensity of these exchanges or relationships during a lifetime bear no relation to their importance. I know that you understand that there is no truth in coincidences and random events. It is, therefore, often not seen or understood at the time of these lesser, for lack of a better description, exchanges, how well planned and significant these events truly are.

Each lifetime is filled with a multitude of meetings and exchanges of energy between what may most often be viewed as strangers. Please know that no soul who crosses the path of an incarnated soul is a stranger. Each and every soul who chooses to incarnate during the lifetime of another also has chosen the timing of their incarnation with purpose and planning. It is also so chosen and planned to interact with the energies of each and every place upon which a soul will tread, and the energies of these places exert a prearranged influence upon the journey of souls within their sphere of influence. It is also so planned by and between all members of the nonhuman kingdoms to share and exchange energies and experiences with each soul that they encounter. Whether a beloved pet, a fragrant flower, a food source, a shelter from a storm, or the storm itself, none of the interactions are random. Each provides or denies a service or lesson as required by the plan of the lifetime, regardless of whether or not this exchange is recognized or accepted at the time of its occurrence.

I remind you once again that these exchanges are neither random nor trivial. Very many of these provide markers along a path, or encouragement at a time of weariness, or many other elements crucial to the unfolding or the progress of the lesson or experience of which they are an integral part. Many serve only as markers or guideposts along the journey by evoking a memory or an emotion that is important to the perspective of the journeying soul. Many also serve the soul as deterrents or warnings, should the participants risk venturing too far from their path and risk losing their way. Many serve as an agent of acceleration or an agent of peace to either charge or temper the experience in which they participate. Many carry messages or guidance to the soul, as agreed during the planning process. Some very few are heaven sent to intervene during an event or series of events that present an element of danger, or to send comfort when a lesson has become too harsh or too gentle to elicit the learning the soul desires. And so, each plays its part faithfully *and* not randomly. This may seem quite complex and yet it is not. Each element of an energy exchange both gives and receives, in some measure, from these exchanges in a manner that aids their own advancement and evolution.

Please remember that when a brave soul chooses to incarnate, it also accepts the limitations of the physical and material. Inside of these limitations, much of the power and knowledge of the soul is hidden from its view. Much of its memory of what exists outside of a physical plane, as well as much of its awareness of what truly exists within a physical plane, will be veiled or hidden from the soul, lying out of its reach much like a hidden treasure waiting to be found once the seeker remembers to awaken and begin the search.

For now I leave you in love and peace.

Rashka, March 25 - 26, 2012.

I am here. I am so glad to be with you again. I am happy to be of service in this matter. Shall we continue our discussion?

I know that many who seek to understand the meaning of their experiences while incarnate have difficulty with the concept of choice and cooperation underlying traumatic situations and events. I do not mean to sound even a tiny bit disrespectful as we discuss this lack of understanding, but I feel that I must state the obvious. These choices are not understood by the mind of humans, except as a result of a serious process of thought in defiance of logic, but the premise is fully understood and accepted by the soul, or the higher self, without need to apply logic to the circumstance. The purest path to understanding of these concepts is one that excludes judgment of all kinds, especially judgment of good and evil. The difficulty herein lies in the human context of polarity, which is very strong in a physical dimension.

Dark and light; right and wrong; victim and oppressor; life and death; past and future; and an innumerable amount of other contrasts and opposites, are so deeply ingrained in the structure of that world that they can be nearly impossible to overcome or ignore. I guess it bears repeating that these structures, limitations, and illusions are created with intent; that they serve the learning process, rather than hindering it, because it is such a grand accomplishment for a human being human to learn to see the divine in a world that gives every appearance of being otherwise. The point of each lesson chosen within a lifetime is to fully experience the journey, not to be content with the arrival at the end of the road, but to place one's feet upon each path as firmly and confidently as possible under the existing conditions of both the road and the traveler, until the start of a new road leads onward to another journey.

Each and all journeys tend to end quite near where they began. It is only the awareness of this circular nature of life that often stays hidden from view while on the path, but is much more easily seen from above, were the traveler able to rise above the travails of the path and look up or down upon their route instead of focusing ahead or behind. Inability to view a human life and its shape and purpose from the viewpoint of a spiritual being is not a failure. These barriers are purposely designed to allow for the fullest experiencing of the physical from within the physical.

Many times, these physical limitations are very nearly the entire purpose of a choice to incarnate. The lesson of learning to feel separation from the whole; or the lesson of learning to believe in the unseen and unproven; the lesson of experiencing both love and a perceived loss of love; the lesson of feeling deep emotions of pain and sorrow; and many other lessons of these kinds, are only possible within the restrictions and limitations of a human existence, and are most often sought because of the bravery and strength required to endure conditions that simply do not exist within the love and completeness of spirit.

It is said that god created man in his own image so that god might see himself reflected in another. While this is not complete and true, I will use this concept as a base for understanding how a soul existing in a state of wholeness and unity could send forth a part of itself into a state that had the illusion of separation, that it might learn both the feeling of separation and remember the truth of unity. Can you understand how value could be gained from illness overcome to return to a state of health, that *this* could add depth and texture that would be missing from a state of continued health? And so it is the same with a state of loneliness and a state of communion, or a state of fear and a state of security. Is not the returning light enhanced by the presence of a period of darkness? Can you understand, then, why a state of joy and love is fuller for having experienced pain and suffering?

Please remember that any state of being that is not fully love, unity, and acceptance is only an illusion, only a part of the whole that is deemed to be set apart, while in truth it is not, because once this state is once *again* reunited with the whole, the experience it contains is lost.

When we continue, let us discuss acceptance and forgiveness as they apply to a human incarnation. I think that you will find this of interest. Until then, beloved, I am your friend and servant.

Rashka, April 4, 2012

I am here. Thank you for taking the time again so soon to speak with me. I am glad to be in your presence. Let us continue.

Among the lessons large and small chosen in the life planning process, the most popular, if that is an appropriate term, is the experiencing of the physical dimension within the limitations created by inhabiting a physical body. Outside of a physical dimension, a soul can choose to inhabit a body, but it is really more of a body composed of light, rather than a body comprised of matter, and the limitations of the physical senses is not present in this state. Also missing from a light body, which in itself is truly only a holographic structure, are the limitations of communication created by language, as well as the limitation of perspective caused by the ego. It is also true that the experiences of the physical senses in relation to others, as part of a physical incarnation, are much sought by evolving souls. Humans take for granted the effects of the physical senses, the auditory and tactile communications and interactions with other physical beings, and these are often missed by a returning soul, as they are remembered with great joy.

Many who incarnate choose to evolve the emotional responses that are so prevalent in a physical dimension. In spirit, all emotion is also whole and complete, and this unified emotional state is love. When in a physical lifetime, the emotions, as is the essence of the soul, appear to be separable into smaller parts of the whole. Much as a prism seems to divide light into various colors by separating the light spectrum, so does a physical incarnation seem to divide or separate love into different emotions. The experience of feeling and observing these pieces of love is also much sought out by an evolving soul, as these seemingly separate emotions do not stand outside of the wholeness of love outside of a physical dimension.

Much as your science classes teach students about a frog by examining the parts of a frog, an evolving soul studies love, and thus itself, by examining its parts. While a soul often plans to participate in as much emotion as it can design into a human lifetime, this is the element of life experience that is most responsible for lifetime after lifetime in a human form, because the range of emotion to be experienced is so large. Also, much like the physical senses, these emotions are remembered fondly when the soul returns home and a desire to re-experience emotions so remembered often lures a soul back to another incarnation.

Please remember that the classification of emotions and experiences into good and bad, difficult and kind, or joyful or sad, are human concepts. The soul holds no such judgments and will remember each as a gift.

And so, then, I will, as promised, return to the topic of acceptance and forgiveness as soul lessons. Because unified and complete beings are interconnected, peaceful, and exist in a state of love, acceptance is natural to a soul. No part of All That Is looks upon any other part of All That Is as less than perfect. Unconditional love is the way and the fabric of the universe. Souls do not strive to learn acceptance and forgiveness, humans do. The (**human**) concept of acceptance implies that one learns to love another as the other is, but that implies that the other contains or exhibits imperfections that must be overlooked. Acceptance seems, to a human being, to be an honorable act and while it is much more noble than many other human acts, it still contains seeds of dishonor. It is, however, still much more subtle than forgiveness.

Again, humans being human strive to forgive another and deem this an honorable act. It, too, is much more honorable than many other human acts, but forgiveness falls short of acceptance and is further yet from unconditional love. Forgiveness is not an act of kindness to another. It is an act performed for the benefit of he who forgives. One does not truly learn through forgiveness, instead one only soothes his own wounds. The underlying theme of forgiveness is that a human will rise above or stifle his own emotions in order to bestow his forgiveness upon another whom he has judged to be inferior or flawed in spirit or deed. The underlying concept of acceptance is kinder only in that one will choose to attempt to understand the feelings of another soul, event, or circumstance that it has deemed to be unsatisfactory or unacceptable. Failing the reaching of enough understanding to accept, a human will instead attempt to forgive. Admittedly, either acceptance or forgiveness is far removed from hate or fear, but both are also far removed from love. Do you understand? There is a great deal of difference, as you know, between 'I have learned to love you despite your shortcomings', 'I love you even though you are … insert flaw of choice here …', and "I love you because you are wonderful and perfect'.

Can you see how it could take many lifetimes and many experiences for a soul pretending to be human to advance through even these three phases of love? Can you imagine how many lifetimes and experiences it could take for a soul pretending to be human to evolve from the emotions of hate and fear to the lesson of acceptance? It requires many, many plans between many, many souls to advance along this (one) path alone; and there are many other lessons and paths to be learned and walked as humans. This reason lies beneath the intricacy of the life planning process. Yet, the complexity belies the simplicity of the process. I, as a part of All That Is, choose, out of love and respect for you, as a part of All That Is, to serve you in your desire to evolve, as you serve me out of love and respect.

I am your friend, Rashka, and it is my pleasure to serve you.

Rashka, April 5, 2012

My thoughts upon completion of this channel:

To err is human. To forgive is human. To love is divine.

I am here. I am happy to be of service. Let us again resume our discussion of the life planning process.

Those souls incarnate within a physical plane who are given the most difficult of lessons, either by choice or as a participant in the choices of a beloved, are, as you have suspected, often also given the gift of remembrance of pieces of home. This is done to fortify them along a rocky path, and is evidenced as second sight, or planned visits home, or is conveyed to them at critical junctures along their journeys. A soul who incarnates into a physical plane without the element of free choice or one who has chosen a gentle walk through a physical lifetime has no need of such aid and, so, instances of these gifts and remembrances are rare among these souls. Once again, I will remind you that no judgment is ever applied to the relative ease or difficulty of a soul's journey or purpose that is played out during an incarnation. The celebration upon the return home of any soul from any such adventure, without regard to its length or intensity, is just as grand.

Each experience carried back home is shared and honored. Does not a mother love her child who misbehaves equally as much as one who does not, especially when the child was born with the intent to expand itself through misbehavior and the mother welcomed the child to learn to expand her grace and patience? When they meet again at home, both mother and child will be overjoyed at the meeting and will laugh heartily at the shared adventure.

And so it is with all souls who choose to share a lifetime in any manner and to any degree. Without exception, the reunion of the souls will be filled with joy and gratitude for the service of each to the other, for at home the plan is remembered and each again knows the other in the fullness of their being. There is no less gratitude for love, respect, or guidance denied than for love, respect, or guidance given, as both were planned and executed from a place of love.

Let us discuss for a moment, if we can, the path of the unawakened human. We have earlier spoken of the desire of many souls to experience the physical planes solely for the purpose of experiencing physicality. We have also spoken of souls who choose and plan a path of slow, gentle evolution. Both of these types of life plans are valuable and honorable. Much of value is gained along both of these paths. The perceived contrasts between those who strive for rapid, intense evolution, those who seek evolution in a calmer, more reserved fashion, and those who seem to slumber through a lifetime are human, third dimensional, types of judgment only. Neither is better. Neither is worse. Each represents an individual choice of pace for a single human lifetime or a series of human lifetimes.

It is neither true nor untrue that a wiser soul chooses any particular path or speed of experience in order to learn. Often it occurs that a wise soul engaged in a fierce pace of exposure to learning within a lifetime will allow within its plan for a change of course to a gentler path at a point in its journey. Often the opposite is true and a wise soul will allow within its plan for an acceleration of the pace of its experiences as it nears a point of resolution. Often a wise soul who slumbers decides to exercise its option to awaken. Just as often a wise soul will choose to slumber as respite from experiences that require too high a level of awareness. All are wise souls and all are free to choose.

Much human suffering has its roots in the perceived loss of someone or something that it holds dear. While this can seem to be a harsh lesson, please remember that all lessons spring from a plan designed to fulfill the wishes of the planner. Please also remember that the duration of a human lifetime is but a breath in the life of the soul. Please remember that no one and no thing is ever lost. Even those who depart a lifetime suddenly have not truly left, they only step outside of the range of perception of those who remain, and even then only for the brief period of time that encompasses a human lifetime. Those who stay with an incarnated soul until the final curtain drops do so out of love. Those who exit during the first act do so out of love. When all are reunited at home the plan will again be remembered and the pain of the loss will dissipate in a flood of love at the reunion. Truly.

For now, please remember how you are loved.

Rashka, April 7, 2012

Chapter Three

SIGNS OF CHANGE

I am here. I am your teacher Isahal and I am glad to be with you once again. You have been spending your time well by staying in communication with spirit. I am happy that it is again my turn to speak.

If we may, I would like to begin a discussion of more practical matters related to the changes occurring in that place. I hope these will be of benefit to you and to those with whom you share these writings and I offer these discussions to comfort and to confirm the progress being made toward ascension. There are many subjects to address and choosing a place to begin is relatively unimportant, as I know you to be a faithful listener.

So much that will be regaining balance as the vibrations of that place increase in speed has already begun to change and yet there seems to be so much frustration and conflict in the forefront around these issues. Please know that this state does not indicate any inclination toward reversal of the path of change. It is human nature to be insecure and fearful in the face of change, even when the change is for the betterment of all concerned. When more of the true nature of the earth and the divine are exposed, this insecurity will disappear.

The process of change has been as gentle as possible up to this point, for precisely this reason, to allow for a slow, sure flushing out of fear. While this may seem to be an increase in fearfulness, the opposite is true. The fear is being loosened from the fearful and is being released into the ethers. We now approach a crossroads of sorts where fear is leaving room for acceptance and that is significant indeed. Acceptance of change leads naturally to surrender of urges to control environments and outcomes. From the position of acceptance and surrender, clearer and more effective action and reaction is possible. Fear and violence were inhabitants of the darkness and the density of the old earth, and are being released at a much more rapid pace at this time. The acts of violence and the resurgence of unrest, rather than being a reflection of continued darkness, are actually serving the entry of the light. Once again, things are not always as they appear. Please consider that perpetrators and victims alike have chosen this service to the greater good and what appear to be injustices and workings of madmen are not. As an example, let us discuss recent wars of large scale that have precipitated great change in earth's recent history.

The civil war in the Americas was one such example. History looks back on this time with regret for the staggering loss of life during this conflict but, as is usually the case, history's version of the story contains little of the real truth. Many souls who incarnated during the current age of change were also participants in the era of the civil war. This may help explain its popularity, if I may use that term to describe an increased affinity for civil war history among so many humans alive today.

It is generally true that an affinity with an event or a time period other than that in which a person is living is an indicator that that soul also shares an incarnation that included that event or era and shares lessons or areas of service in both lifetimes. These associations, when recognized, can help shed light upon the path of the soul engaged in this attraction to another time and there is generally a correlation between the importance of the associated lesson to the level of interest or obsession with the historical period or event.

The time of the civil war was also a period of clearing of heavier, denser energies that preceded a time of great change. The era that succeeded the civil war included not only important changes related to individual freedom, but also included great technological changes that would, over the following century, transform much of the world's societies. Spiritual progress is much more accessible in circumstances where less emphasis needs to be focused on survival and the freeing of hands and minds from the labor and rigor of matters of survival creates the opportunity for the leisure activities of education, research, philosophy, and matters of the mind and soul to grow as the matters of the body lessen in lives. Technologies followed this period of warfare that changed greatly the arenas of work, agriculture, medicine, and education, among others, that could not take a foothold in the pre-war culture.

And so it follows that again the period of the world wars served much the same function. Energies were released in immense quantities across vast expanses of the earth as these conflicts raged. While history views these periods of war as justified actions of defense against political and religious acts of injustice righted by first a 'war to end all wars' and again by its companion the 'great war', in fact both events were again acts of energy clearing and change planned and willingly engaged in by souls advancing the evolution of humankind toward ascension. The age of unity and peace that dawns in the current days would have been impossible without the release of density accomplished during these periods of war and the end of the second of these world wars marks the true beginning of the shift of the ages.

Many souls who departed during these wars returned very quickly to earth in large numbers to again participate in the changes that they had helped to begin. So successful were their acts and sacrifices that another great war of retribution, that had been planned to complete the clearing process, was rendered unnecessary, granting relief from the prophesied Armageddon designed as a final desperate attempt to remove the darkness and allow the entry of the light upon the earth once again.

It then follows that because the energy releases required at the end of the age were accomplished by and through the acts of mankind, it was also no longer necessary for the earth to participate in cataclysmic changes to her planetary body to affect these energy releases. This has allowed her to perform these physical energetic releases and adjustments in a manner much more to her liking and has resulted in much less damage to her inhabitants than would have been required under the original plan of ascension.

And yet, these accomplishments both grand and miraculous appear to go unrecognized in their truth. Humans, in the process of behaving quite humanly, point to acts of violence and fear as proof of impending doom. With their minds so occupied, they do not notice large and devastating acts of violence and fear that are avoided and do not point to them as proof of impending salvation.

Let us speak again soon, my friend. Remember how much you are loved. Remember who you are.

Isahal, August 16, 2012

I am here. I am your friend and guide Rashka and I am happy to be speaking with you this day. The teacher Isahal sends his love and asks that you speak with him again soon, but for today I would like to speak with you, if I may.

There is much that is of interest to you about the shift and we are glad to share knowledge with you on this subject, as it will be helpful for all souls involved to awaken memories of home as these changes transpire. It will ease the transition because so many have adjusted so well to the circumstances of life behind the veil and as it lifts there will be less effort required to adjust with more awareness of the truth of the world and the heavens remembered. This is good work and we are happy to help.

Let us discuss more of the mechanics of the old earth and the new earth. As you are aware, the properties of a physical dimension are unique among the universes because of the material nature of these dimensions. Energy and matter are one and the same, but this is much less evident in a physical world. This is a result, in part, of the physical limitations included in the construction of these dimensions and is also a result of the limited perception, generally, of its inhabitants. I will again state an obvious point that outside of a physical world matter has no need to manifest as matter. Therefore, in other dimensions all energy holds to a purer form. I say that this is an obvious point, but if one holds the illusion that all that can be seen, heard, felt, and measured comprises the totality of all that exists, as it does for many beings engaged in a physical world, this point would not be as obvious as it would be to a being aware of the possibility of the existence of the unseen properties of the world and the universe. The limited perception that is experienced in a physical world is chosen, as we have discussed before, purposefully and the lack of awareness of all the rest is not a shortcoming of an incarnated soul, but is rather an indicator that the soul is fully engaged in the circumstances of that lifetime and that world.

Others are able to imagine a different world and others are able to perceive a different world. To each, the world in which they are engaged is every bit as valid and real. As the physical dimension opens to allow the overlaying of the other dimensions to be available to their perception, this will necessitate adjustments to be made by the participants. This process will be easy for some and more difficult for others. All possible care and guidance will be available to ease these transitions.

We are very excited about this process as it has not been designed before in this manner, to make the adjustments while so many are still incarnate. I am sure you could understand how it would be simpler, in a way, to wait until the incarnate beings had returned home before the energetic changes are made and to then repopulate the world under the new energetic structure. It speaks very highly of the creativity and the strength of the souls involved that this change is being made as it is.

When matter is formed from energy it holds a physical form by creating electromagnetic grids or structures. The electromagnetic energy, which is part of the pure energy that is diverted or converted, exerts itself upon the energy not so occupied to slow the rate of vibration of the energy. This process allows a very small part of this energy to seem to be material in form. The rest of the energy remains connected to the material, but holds a vibratory rate that is slightly higher and is thus not visible. What appears to be empty space between the particles of matter is anything but empty. Within these seemingly empty spaces exists all of the rest of the universe: alive, active, and cognizant of the whole of itself. When we speak of the blending of the dimensions, we are actually referring to the exposure of more of the energetic structure that has been unseen.

The revelation of the unseen is the outcome of the shift into the new age of the physical world. In order to accomplish this transition, it will be necessary only to raise the vibration level of the material component of the energy already present by a minutia and the energetic grids or systems have been prepared for this shift in vibration. The levels of vibration being restored have been utilized in that place before the choice was made to create a denser, more material, plane and will be remembered when they return in very short order by the souls who are willing to accept the unseen as real. There will be a slightly longer period of adjustment required for those very deeply invested in the physicality of the world. Please be assured that all necessary preparations have been established to guide these souls through the transition. Great care has been taken by the guides of all souls to ensure their capability to transition through this change. Those souls who make the informed choice to avoid these physical and energetic changes will be welcomed home with all due honor and respect.

As in the past, the material aspect of that dimension will be lighter and less dense after the increase of the vibrational rate is fully accomplished, but the material nature of the dimension will remain. It will be the spiritual aspect of the physical dimension that will exhibit the most change as more of the truth of spirit and energy reveals itself.

Rashka, August 19, 2012

I am here. I am glad to be with you again, my friend. Let us continue our previous discussion of the changes to the material world that are occurring and that will occur in the very near future.

As the vibrational rate of that physical dimension rises, the most profound changes will be to the spiritual beliefs of the souls living within the dimension. Within these higher vibrations much will be revealed in its truth that will change the way humans see themselves and others. We are very excited to see the mass awakening to the true nature of life that these changes will bring. It will no longer be possible, as it has been for a long time in earth time, to experience the separation from all of life. It has been a part of the physical design of that dimension to hide divinity from the souls who incarnated there so that they might learn of divinity from outside of the comfort and love of the unified All That Is essence.

There has been a longstanding argument in that place among men of science and men of religion over the effect of knowing that alien life existed outside of that planet and whether or not such knowledge would incite fear or wonder. This discussion has been good practice for the real question, which has always been how men would react to the existence of the divine within and without the planet. The answer is that the revelation of the omnipresent divinity of all that exists changes everything.

It is truly this spiritual truth that returns heaven to earth. Within this knowing none can be separate and none can be feared. None can be treated as material, disposable, or unworthy when the light of the divine is finally seen to emanate from each living being. It will be the light; visible at long last, that will teach the truth of all life. As you remember, light is merely an expression of love and the revelation of the light will allow the senses of humans to both see and feel the love contained in themselves and in all other beings. Light dispels darkness and love dispels fear. Those who hold no fear do not hate. Those who hold no fear do not hoard. Those who hold no fear do not shame.

We have been waiting patiently for this time of change and are truly excited to see these miraculous changes unfold. So many have chosen to incarnate during this shift in anticipation of being able to embody the wonder and the miracles of this new earth! As a reward, of sorts, for their service to their divinity they will be present during the ascension of a physical world, a change as yet unknown throughout the universe.

As the new world is revealed, the truth of the old world will also be revealed and released. In seeing the plan and the purpose of the old world, there will be healing of all that was carried as wounds and hurt. The truth of all will be seen and felt in each moment. The beauty of all will be seen at last. The world will replace all division and struggle with unity and cooperation and it will once again be seen to be the wonderful world that it has been all along.

We can hardly wait a moment more, but please know that there will be more moments as the changes are established in the most graceful manner possible. Hold to your faith. All is as I say, as it would not be possible for me to be untrue to you, my beloved.

Rashka, August 25, 2012

I am here. I am called Isahal. I am glad to be speaking with you once again. Thank you for taking the time to speak with me this day. We have been speaking of the changes in progress at the end of the current age and the dawn of the new age and I would propose that we continue our discussion on this topic.

As the end of the old world approaches with all due haste, there are several aspects of the old world that are being removed, as they are no longer necessary. Among these departing aspects are karma debts. Creation and balancing of karmic debt was a learning tool under the paradigm that passes away. Also leaving the energy of that world are other experiences that focus on opposites and polarity, such as concepts of good and evil and lack and greed, to name only a couple. It would bear consideration at this time to watch for signs of crumbling within the structure of all establishments and institutions that exhibit and encourage polarity, as they prepare for the completion of their service and the dismantling of their influence upon the affairs of mankind. Also leaving will be more mechanical functions established within cultures and processes, such as cause and effect, aging and disease, and chemical and heat induced material processes.

All of these functions have also served a purpose within a denser environment, but will not align with higher vibrations that arrive in each new moment. As these higher vibratory rates begin to take hold within that physical dimension, all functions and institutions that are out of alignment with the energies of the new world will simply return to their natural state and will seem to disappear. The act of removal is less of a process of destruction of existing elements of the old earth that no longer serve than it will be a process of transmutation into different, lighter elements that will serve or, as it will be in many cases, a return to basic energetic forms that will later serve other purposes in other places.

As we are discussing signs of the impending change I would suggest examination of the basis of the function of systems and institutions as well as physical processes and structures with an eye upon whether they serve or support unity or polarity.

There need be no fear or concern for consequences of these removals for, as I have mentioned earlier, cause and effect will no longer apply in the new vibration and structure of the new earth. All that will be required, as they pass out of that place, will be gratitude for their presence and a blessing for the gifts they have bestowed in the course of their service. As you are aware, gratitude for blessings of good effect are powerful acts, but gratitude for blessings of ill effect are signs of mastery.

We have much to discuss on this topic and so I suggest that this communication serve only as an introduction to this topic and request, if it pleases you, that we again meet over a course of days to illuminate our subjects in depth. I am grateful for your attention and your service and look forward to our next meeting. Your friend and teacher,

Isahal, August 27, 2012

I am here. I am called by the name of Isahal and I am grateful for your presence and your commitment. I would like to continue our previous discussion for a while, if we may. Thank you.

As we discussed earlier, there will be many energies departing with the arrival of the new vibrations. These energies functioned beautifully and purposefully in the old earth dimensions, but they do not resonate with the vibrations of the new earth, so their presence will no longer be evident after the shift is complete. Even as we speak, the influence of some of these energies have nearly lost effectiveness while others will continue to diminish as they are overlain with new energetic systems that resonate with the new earth.

For today, let us begin our discussion with the energy fields or grids of karma, as these have been the first of the old energies to resolve their function and leave the earth plane. Nearly simultaneously with the commitment to ascend the earth and her inhabitants from within the physical plane, the service of karmic balancing was fulfilled. If I may, let me offer an explanation of the function and purpose of karma to the old earth and perhaps this will help you understand why its presence in that plane is no longer necessary.

In the times of the darker, denser earth, there was no plan for change or return to the lighter state of the new earth yet formed. In those times, souls were drawn to the physical planes by experiences that were unique to such a plane and were easiest to play out in the density of a third dimensional world. Much was learned and much was experienced by the souls who incarnated and the others who visited this plane while disincarnate and all functioned according to plan. Over time it came to be believed by humans that this world would remain in this state of density and dimness until, through some form of catastrophic event, the planet was cleansed and cleared of density and a new game board, of sorts, could be set. From this perspective, there seemed to be little reason to continue incarnations without much in the way of new challenges for souls seeking elevation and evolution. It was from this point of boredom or impatience that the energies of karma were born. Under the influence of the karmic grids, a state of imbalance was created by the interactions of incarnated souls that carried forward from their acts of love or their withholding of love between the souls. This imbalance, in effect, bound these souls to one another during and after the lifetime that they shared, much as positive and negative magnetic charges bind atoms and molecules in a form that balances their charges. This is necessary under the laws of earthly physics; however, universal laws make no such allowances for a state of imbalance.

So it was that a soul with a positive karmic charge was bound to a soul with a negative karmic balance so that a state of balance could be returned to them in combination. I do not mean to oversimplify this circumstance by giving the impression that these states of balance were equally balanced between two souls. Achieving the state of perfect balance of karmic energy often involved many souls, each of whom contributed their share in unequal amounts of positive and negative karma charges, until a state of perfect balance was achieved. This function of karma contributed to the fluid nature of soul groups, as when a particular soul chose to join a different soul group for a new experience it was necessary that his energetic charge to the soul group be replaced by adding another soul who carried a similar charge. The addition of the component of maintaining a proper karmic balance of a group of souls throughout the course of an incarnation thus created an interesting new aspect to the act of incarnation and this was very good. Do you understand? Good.

Let us move forward then. As the elements of the shift began to be established within the physical plane in which the earth is contained, there began a lessening of the density of that place. With these changes there came changes in the physical laws of mechanics and physics. I ask you to consider that fairly recent discoveries within the physical sciences might have been initiated less by newly inspired scientists and mathematicians than by actual changes in the physical properties under their study, made all the more visible and measurable by the lessened density and not an effect of advanced technology. Humans love to hitch the cart to the horse in opposite order and revel in their own clever creations and such antics bring us great joy and much laughter.

In any case, as the density began to decrease in the earth plane the delicate balance of the karmic energies could no longer be maintained and they saw that their purpose of maintaining balance was not needed in a general state of natural balance and unity. And so it was decided that as the density was lightened, the karmic energies would be released in equal share until such time as they were no more within that plane, and this threshold was crossed. So too will it be for each of the energetic systems and structures contained within our topic of discussion.

Let us pause at this point, if it suits you, and approach another example when again we speak. I leave you in love.

Isahal, August 29, 2012

I am here. I am your friend and teacher Isahal and I am glad once again to be in your presence. Let us continue.

Among the vestiges of the old world preparing to lose their influence within the structure of the new earth are systems based in polarity; such as good and evil, rich and poor, and worthy and worthless. Again, all such systems and the institutions upon which the formation and foundation hold to and spring from these bases will not serve in the new vibrations of unity. The most severe, and perhaps the most obvious, institutions will weaken the fastest, but all whose foundations stand on inequality and differentiation will, in time, follow.

In the old earth the illusion of separation from the whole, where there seemed to be parts and pieces of any structure, being, or institution that stood apart from others of its kind, was designed to teach the truth of the oneness of all. It might not seem logical at first, but in practice the lack of any aspect of the whole, even though such lack was only illusionary, encouraged the search for the rest. If fully effective, the goal at the end of any soul's hero's journey to find unity was the exposure of the illusion and release from the burden of lack associated with the illusion. Perhaps it will help to state an example for clarification.

Suppose that an honorable and just man finds himself engrossed in a world of evil and injustice and instead of adapting to his surroundings for ease of travel through this place he instead chooses to hold to a belief, a dream, or a remembrance of a world filled with good. If he is strong and sure of his own heart, he seeks evidence of goodness and strives for a just life in all that he undertakes. Against all odds, with no company in his quests for good, success is measured not by the amount of evidence that he gathers on his journey, but is measured instead by his devotion to the wisdom of his own soul. This is a valiant course to set and a wondrous act of faith and hope that holds him to his course, come what may. Can you see how the knowledge of his own power and commitment would not have been gained in a world where goodness and justice prevailed? The learning comes to such a brave soul through the process of experiencing a world of a different kind and coming to know evil and injustice and refusing to bend to their influence, but instead seeking out the qualities that they mask as though not connected to the whole of good and evil or justice and injustice.

Each element that is based in polarity only seems to be less than the whole, in truth it is not, but for the purpose of enriching and evolving souls each end of the pole pretends to be a part or apart. Do you understand? I will tell you now that as the vibration of the energies of which that plane is composed adjust and rise; the truth of these things will again be seen and remembered. Their connections and interdependence will be evident and in that moment the polarity based structures will no longer serve. They will return to their state of unity and exhibit their truth once again. As they had seemed to exist separately in the old world, so will they seem not to exist in the new. It will not truly be any of these institutions and systems that change. They were never really separate in the first place. It will only be the perception of them that will change.

Isahal, September 2, 2012

I am here. I am called by the name of Isahal. I am happy to be with you again. We have been discussing the signs of change from the old earth to the new earth. Perhaps most important among the changes occurring at this time is the return to the earth of conscience and accountability. I know that you have always felt the absence of conscience among the workings of the affairs of man, and so I thought that it may bring you comfort to know that this aspect is being strengthened under the new energy structure.

It has been a function of the illusion of separation that was manifest upon the earth that it seemed as though any single human or group of humans could operate as though the interests of self were more important than the interests of all. As the energy grids are realigned to reveal the unity and interdependence of all of life it will no longer be possible to maintain the illusion that any action or decision that benefits one while not benefitting others is acceptable. In reality, any action that denies, withholds, or harms another is an act performed against the self, because the self and the whole are one and the same.

It will soon be revealed that actions and decisions that both benefit and include the whole will be the only kind of action or decision that will be sustainable within the new energy. Any other kind of action or decision will not function within the framework of the physical plane. This particularly applies to the creation and manifestation of the material from the energetic. I like the example that you remembered and it bears acknowledgement. When you were a child in school, a teacher asked a student who had brought gum to class if he had brought enough for everyone. If he had not enough to share with every other student, then he was not allowed to keep the gum. It will be very similar in the new earth. It has never been more difficult to create enough for everyone than it was to create enough for only a few and the students of the earth shall quickly learn this lesson and learn to apply it to the new world.

As the energy vibrations change to a higher state of vibration, this lesson will begin to be displayed. It is an important lesson and so it will become very obvious very quickly. Each man is his brother's keeper and all men are brothers. Those who exhibit behavior that is contrary to this basic truth will very quickly see their efforts fail and this process has already begun. Those who create and share their bounty will be rewarded with an increase in the fruits of their creation. Those who do not share will suffer loss of their hoard, be it possessions, money, or power. Unless it is created with the intent of benefitting all, it will not remain. Those who have operated their lives in ill will shall very soon be found to be dependent upon the good will of others. As I have said, it is an easy lesson and will be quickly learned.

Good always fosters good; therefore, good intent fosters good results. There never has been a limitation of the resources available within that plane and that will not change. In love and from love all things are possible. In the new earth all that is done in love and from love will be certain.

Let us speak again soon, my friend.

Isahal, September 12, 2012

I am here. I am called by the name of Sarassa. We have spoken in the past and I am happy to be in your presence once again. I have come forth this day to talk to you about heaven. I believe that you will find this interesting in light of the impending and rapidly progressing return of heaven to the earth. I hope that this topic pleases you.

All who walk the planet know heaven in their hearts, but their minds generally forget heaven as they adjust to an earthly life. This is for the best, as the earth serves to teach lessons of earthly life and too much of a remembrance of heaven generally would interfere with the chosen lessons. As always, there are exceptions. The beloved children remember heaven for a while so that the harshness of that place does not cause them to run from life. So much would be gained by listening to the children when they talk of heaven and some have learned to listen. Please remember that by the time that the children learn language much of that which they would relate has been forgotten. As the new time without time approaches, many more children will retain much more of heaven and those around them shall remember to listen without the burden of language, with their hearts and not their ears, and this shall ease their way. It shall, as you have guessed, also allow many of the children and young adults who have withdrawn inward to also be heard and healed.

If the children could be heard, they would talk of heaven in terms of love, light, color, and sound. Heaven is both a dimension that unifies all other dimensions and it is a dimension of creativity. Each and all souls resident in heaven contribute to its design and form. While not material in nature, it may very well be experienced *as material*, should a soul desire such, because heaven encompasses and includes material as well as non-physical dimensions. Any aspects of its component dimensions are available for the creative expression of its residents. The most beloved aspects of the universe in the way of sound and color are amplified in their expression in heaven and it is most often these intensified elements that are remembered by those who glimpse heaven in dreams, meditations, or astral visits.

As your friend the teacher has told you, there are increasing signs of heaven appearing on the earth. Among these signs will be noticeable changes in light, color, and musical tones. These increasingly vibrant colors and more complex musical sounds shall serve as reminders of heaven to the hearts of men and shall be both proof and comfort in the days to come. Watch also for visible and measurable changes in light, which shall bring a sense of motion and life to the light that enters that world, especially after the time of the alignment with the great central sun. This alignment shall cause a merging of the lights of the two suns and the light itself shall expand its dimensionality to exhibit more of the truth of its nature. Some of the wondrous beings and energies present within the light of heaven shall be exposed and this too shall spark remembrances of heaven.

Please remember that heaven and earth are one. They always have been. The veil of forgetfulness has served its purposes well in keeping heaven hidden and its removal shall bring much joy to the world and to heaven.

Please also remember that heaven is not a place, but is rather a state of being to which all men return. For now, I leave you in peace and love until we speak again.

Sarassa, September 15, 2012

Chapter Four

SOUL GROUPS AND FAMILIES

Thank you for waiting. I am called by the name of Michaline. I am of the family of Michael the Protector and I serve Sarah as guide and protector, as I have done for many lifetimes in the past. I am honored that you asked to speak with me on her behalf and I am honored that Sarah wishes to hear from us also.

I am certain that it will take no one among you by surprise that Sarah is a member of the soul group of the family of Michael the Protector; that it has been her place and purpose in many lives to be a defender of the downtrodden and a protector of the weak and the ill. While it is a difficult path that is walked by those who choose to live a life of misery and limited physical stamina, it would be a nearly impassable road without the aid and presence of a member of our family nearby in the most dire of situations and during the times of most trial. This is the service that we choose, to defend in ways large and small.

Many families of souls choose a theme of service that is repeated throughout many lives. Some choose their service as a guide or guardian angel. Many choose their service in physical form. Many choose to both guide from this side and to provide a more active role in human form, yet we all serve. Some who serve choose to nurture and comfort. Some choose to teach. Some serve as witnesses and messengers. Some serve by providing contrast and motivation. We serve to protect and to defend. It is not what we do for others; it is who we are at the core of our beings. Many who choose human lifetimes are generalists. They arrive in each new life eager to learn and experience, that they may share their learning and their experiences when they return home. The vast majority of soul families are thus.

While it is true that members of the family of Michael also learn and share their learning and growth with all the rest when they return home, this is not our primary purpose for taking the human journey. We are warriors and protectors first and foremost. Our service is crucial to the growth of others, and the honor of our service drives us. We defend both souls and places. Throughout time it is the family of Michael that has defended the holy lands and the home lands.

(We stopped here for the evening and began again the next evening.)

I am here again. I am glad to be of service to you and to my beloved Sarah. Let us continue.

I am glad that you understand the difference between a maker of war and a protector, as this is a great distinction. I know that it is the purpose of many warriors to engage in war, but this behavior is generally for their own purposes and not for the interests of others, as it is for a protector. Also, there is another distinction between warriors that is very much like the distinction between the implements of war. Most warriors carry both a sword and a shield. A being of war uses the sword primarily and the shield only when necessary; a being of protection uses the shield primarily and the sword only when necessary, and these choices, or outlooks, speak to their purpose and intent. We of the family of Michael also carry both a sword and shield, but we prefer the shield to deflect harm from ourselves and our charges. At times the shield deflects harm and sometimes the shield hides, supports, or fortifies a potential victim of the sword. Sometimes it serves to carry the wounded from the field that they may heal. Oftentimes we serve as the shield ourselves to deflect attacks both small and large. This is a service that carries a great deal of honor and reward for us and does us no permanent harm, as the lending or gifting of strength to another only allows for our strength to be replenished anew.

I know that our dear Sarah holds some pain around her singularity in this life and wonders if she has chosen incorrectly in the past. She has not. She is living true to her purpose and aligned with her calling. A human lifetime is such a short span. She will remember this when we welcome her home, and from here her personal sacrifices will be seen to be small and necessary, while her service will be seen to be great and essential. It is so, and she is loved and respected for her service always. Please ask her to remember that she bears a shield not only for the protection of others. Please ask her to remember to use the shield also to protect herself from doubt and fear. It is a weapon of great power, much more powerful than a sword, and her shield has served her gloriously for much longer than she can now recall and will serve her gloriously for much longer than she can imagine.

She knows not the good service that she has provided to family, friends, and strangers, but we do, and we stand in awe of her accomplishments and her determination, as much as we take pride in her generous nature. Please remind her that a shield not only deflects a blow, it also cushions a fall, for a divine shield is not forged from hardened steel, it is, in fact, fashioned from love and respect made manifest and there is nothing stronger in the world than an implement wielded in love and deployed with respect for the soul of another.

Until we again meet, I leave you in love.

Michaline, May 18, 2012

I am here. I am your friend and sister Rashka. I am always at your service when you have questions and will be glad to discuss the topic of soul families with you. Let us begin with your soul family, of which we are both members, so this topic is one with which I am very familiar. I am glad that you recognized the play of words. You discussed language clues with the teacher recently and this is one such clue. The word familiar is a clue to a family relationship, or a clue to one's family roots or connections. When a place, a situation, or a being feels familiar, that is your wisdom speaking to you as a reminder of who you are.

When this sensation of familiarity is evoked, it is a marker that indicates that you have reached a point along your path where this path and another of significance have crossed, or it is a marker that you have encountered a being who belongs to your soul family, or it contains a message from home that has been left along your path. Much would be gained from taking notice of familiarity.

Let us return to the topic at hand, soul families. First, let me explain that there is a difference between a soul family and a soul group.

A soul group is a subset, if we may define it in mathematical terms, of the entirety of souls that comprise All That Is. This subset, or group of souls, is a fluid collective of souls gathered by and with intent for the fulfillment of a particular goal. I define a soul group as fluid because its components are not fixed and souls are free to go in and leave soul groups at will as it suits the needs of the group, the purpose of the group, or the member soul. Do you recall the diagrams you studied in school that were comprised of intersecting circles? If these diagrams also included circles embedded within other circles and were modeled in more than two dimensions, they would fairly well represent the formation and interaction of soul groups. As with the model described above, you could see that a soul, if defined as a point within this diagram, could occupy multiple circles simultaneously, especially if the dimension of movement were added to each of the circles that comprised the model. I have called this fluidity. Do you understand?

Let us go on, then, to talk about a soul family, if we may. While it is both possible and probable that a member of your soul family may be also a member of your soul group at any given point, the converse is not necessarily true. A soul family carries bonds and commitments that are stronger and of a greater duration, because they are bonds of purpose. Can you understand the difference between a goal and a purpose as it would relate to the time and the commitment required to achieve a goal, versus the time and commitment to a purpose? These stronger, purposeful bonds would represent those of a soul family, while the looser, goal oriented bonds would represent those that bind a soul group to each other. A group of souls will commit to each other for a life, or several lives, until a mutually formed goal is achieved. A soul family will stay committed to each other generally through all lifetimes, bound by their common purpose.

I would like to discuss the particular soul families at length, because it is of interest to you, when you are not as weary, if we may, but I will not leave your question unanswered. Your beloved grandson does, in fact, belong to the family of Gabriel the Messenger and he is also a member of your soul group. Your purpose is broader than his. I hope this answers your question for today. Let us speak again soon, beloved.

Rashka, May 20, 2012

I am here. I am your friend Rashka. I am glad that you wish to speak with me again and am glad to answer your questions, always. May we continue our discussion?

Let us discuss the families of souls further. I am sure that it will be interesting to those humans who are members of these families to find a clue within these pages as to their purposes and life courses as human angels, if we may use that term to describe their service.

I will begin with the family of Gabriel the Messenger, as it holds particular interest to those whom you love so dearly. As the name of this family would indicate, the members of this family serve the world as deliverers of messages from beyond that place and are the storytellers and truth speakers of their societies. This service also pervades the lives of the messengers again and again, and they also serve in small ways and in great ways. They tell of other times and places with what may seem to be grand imaginations, when truly they speak from experience. Their talent or their gift is to know how and when to relay information in a comforting and supportive manner, so that the best result is achieved for the listener. They do not only relate stories and messages, they also gather stories and messages for safekeeping. They can be seen as disarming at times and are fond of words and tales. Because of their lineage, most of their favorite stories will be morality tales or will contain clues to great truths. Often they will utilize a tale only for its intended effect and pay no heed to its truthfulness. This is firmly within the bounds of their mission, as they have an understanding of the creative nature of reality as opposed to the rigid appearance of reality within a physical world. They are correct in their understanding. They are creative. They carry and create stories and messages with solid intent and show little patience for the creation of stories and messages born from malicious intent. They are at home with fantasy while being dedicated to truth and this is not as contradictory as it may at first seem. They bring to the world words of comfort, words of encouragement, words of hope, and lessons of faith, and they possess a sense of perfect timing and genuine understanding of the human condition, as do all human angels. They serve in love and carry great wisdom. Those who encounter them sense that they are special beings and it is an honor to share a lifetime with a member of the family of Gabriel the Messenger. They will always follow a calling to where they are needed and they are always needed where they are.

Let us move on to discuss the family of Uriel the Healer. Members of this family are spiritual or soul healers, which can be quite different from physical healers. Many who consider themselves to be healers in that place are not soul healers and are not members of the family of Uriel the Healer. A spiritual healer understands that all physical ill occupies the physical body only and does not originate there. Therefore, they also understand that the relief, or release, of physical ailments is also not accomplished within the physical form. For this reason, few of the members of this family of healers will be found inside of the medical profession, and I have used the term profession intentionally. Please do not misunderstand. Many members of the medical community provide service to the ill and the dying with great dedication and there is also great honor in their efforts. The members of the family of Uriel the Healer do not treat disease with medicines, bandages, or knives. They do not treat disease at all, really. They lend comfort to the soul and offer love and acceptance to minister to the troubled souls whose physical bodies manifest illness as a sign of a need unmet. Physical illness is not a punishment. Physical illness is not a weakness. Physical illness is by design an impetus for change, growth, or learning, or it is the means by which a soul returns home at the end of a lifetime's journey. Illness often triggers a change of focus or direction in a lifetime, an awakening if you will, or a rededication to a life of purpose when a soul has nearly forgotten its way. Illness is also often chosen along the path to further the learning of another or many others. It is not an enemy to be battled; it is a tool for enlightenment. This is the understanding of a true healer who does not provide relief from the symptoms of illness, but instead provides support and guidance as the lesson and the purpose of the illness is revealed. Some of the finest healers choose to serve through the embodiment of and triumph over illness, injury, or disability, revealing lessons great and small to those who witness the miracle of disease released or lives forever changed by force of will or faith.

Let us continue again soon. For now, my friend, rest and remember how dearly you are loved.

Rashka, May 24, 2012

I am here. I am glad to be speaking with you again. Shall we continue our discussion of soul families?

Let us discuss the family of Raphael the Teacher. Members of this soul family, as are members of the other soul families we have discussed, are dedicated across lifetimes to a common purpose. In the case of the family of Raphael the Teacher, these human angels guide and teach. They are the means by which knowledge is brought into the physical world from the universe for the advancement of civilizations and individual souls. The members of this soul family are patient and gentle souls, as guidance and knowledge offered are not always acknowledged or accepted when presented. The members of this family, because of their purpose, have access to the plans laid for the souls and worlds that they guide and carry a quiet and gentle patience toward evolving souls that most others find difficult to hold. They are often involved in the arts, because so much universal knowledge expresses itself through art in that plane and the arts also provide inspiration and expression of higher goals and truths to the masses without need of individual instruction. These are the human angels who provide a home for ideas when they are introduced into the world. The quiet and solitude of their practices contrast the importance of their service.

Those who understand that they are expressing divine inspiration and do not claim personal genius or talent are of the family of Raphael the Teacher. Those who persist to uphold the truth of universal ideals are of the family of Raphael the Teacher. Those who teach peace and love by example are also of this family. Their reward for their continued service is not within the worlds that they serve, and yet they offer their service again and again for the benefit of others and all. They often seem to be ahead of their time, but they hold a divine concept of time and a peaceful understanding that creation and evolution are processes and not events. They are not outsiders to the societies that they serve, contrary to appearances, because their service as the vessels of creation and knowledge grant them awareness of the importance of their acts of service. Should you be honored to share a lifetime with a member of the family of Raphael the Teacher, know that you have seen the truth of greatness, which is dedication to purpose without ego, and learn as much from this teacher as you can. That is his reward.

Rashka, June 2, 2012

I am here. I am called by the name of Sarassa. We have not yet met, but I am of your group of guides and teachers. I have come at the request of your guide Rashka this day to speak with you about the workings of the heavens. I understand that you are interested in these matters and it will be my pleasure to share my knowledge with you. You asked this day to speak with your guides and angels and I am of the latter kind of being. You would call me a guardian angel, I suppose, as I am assigned to measure and assist in the lessons of incarnate souls. I am of your group and, therefore, it is a part of my course and responsibility to watch over you and yours while you are away from home.

I am pleased to be communicating with you directly in this manner. It seems much more efficient than the usual means of communication, which use whispers and signs or the words of others. I know that you have noticed that I seem to generate no energy signature that you can sense. That is perfectly normal. As an incarnate human you are unaccustomed to the feeling of peace and that is the signature that I carry into your space.

While it may feel like nothing, it is really nearly everything. A state of true peace is divine and that is why so many humans on the path of enlightenment seek to achieve inner peace through prayer or ritual. It offers a glimpse of the divine state of Nirvana. It is a state from which enlightenment is most easily fostered and is, therefore, very different from a state of nothingness. Peace is still and most things that are still are of god more directly and more closely. It is good that you pray for peace for yourself and for others. The stillness of peace creates a place, or a ground work, for the inspiring and the miraculous to anchor within the soul. Peace is an angel's playground, if you will, because it belongs to us also. It is our gift and it is ours to share. So please know that asking for peace invites angels and feeling peaceful acknowledges our presence.

You are very strongly protected and guided in your work by your guardians and your teachers. That is a good thing and is performed out of love and respect. I am here today to tell you that you are also able to reach out to us and to the earth mother and, if you like, directly to your source without concern that the task is too large for you while in the physical and will be received with honor. All souls incarnate possess the ability to speak to the divine, and always have. The ability to receive and understand the response of the divine has, for a long time by earth standards, been granted to only a few. This has no relation to worthiness, as all souls are equally a part of the divine, but the path of those who transcend the earthly for the purpose of touching the divine is chosen by few. Many who have chosen to carry this gift upon the earth have been persecuted and worse for carrying truth into a world built around illusions and lies. So while it is possible for all souls to interact with the divine, it is not always wise and so this gift stays generally among the groups or families of souls who have experience in this art, and it is through the generations of these family members that this skill holds its place upon the earth.

It is said that this gift is hereditary, but that is not factual. The appearance that this skill runs in families is not because of genetic codes, but is rather because families often contain many members of the same soul group. When they enter an incarnate life, soul groups plan to enter together. It is very logical to do so because they share each and every experience of other lives and often share common goals for their journeys into the world. Many of the physical genetic codes that they carry into each lifetime bear such similarity because of their shared experiences, which reflect in their genetic structures. They also help each to identify each other once the veil is placed, as like seeks like and the physical body has an inherent intelligence for recognizing its own family groups.

While much of the structure of communication will be changed as the veil lifts to reveal the new age of earth, the changes will be easiest for those who walk between the worlds and their lessons and examples will be of great assistance to those who have not. It is truth that manifestation must be founded in belief; one cannot create that which it cannot conceive. Each time a soul incarnate opens to the possibility of direct communication with the divine, the basis has been conceived.

I bring you words of encouragement to help keep you on your path and I bring you peace because you are deserving of peace. Please remember to ask and we will always respond to your call. In love I leave you.

Sarassa, August 12, 2012

I am here. I am called by the name of Sarassa. It is wonderful to be speaking with you again. May we continue our previous discussion? Thank you for inviting me to speak with you again.

A discussion of the relationships between souls would be a very fitting topic for today, and it is truly well chosen. Let us begin by reminding ourselves that all that exists contains the divine spark of the creator and is, therefore, essentially connected to all else that exists by and through this divine essence. Although spread throughout creation, each of these sparks or beacons of light are still unified with the source. I can see how difficult the concept might be to grasp, as it is more difficult to describe than I first imagined from within the context of the physical universe where different rules apply. Outside of the physical dimensions there is no distance - no space, therefore, it is normal that any thing or spirit can be all places at once. Even though I have described the divine spark as a part of the creator, it is in truth not only a part, as it would be seen to be inseparable from the whole. For lack of a better description, it is this continuous connection with the creator that unites all life. This concept is very important and I try to take care to translate it properly. Please grant me a little of your patience while I search for the proper words.

I do not want to create the impression that the creator, the mother god, or any created concept, system, or structure is in any way separate from others or from itself, despite the appearance of separation that was created within the design of the physical universes. All That Is exists in a state of oneness, even when it chooses to believe otherwise.

As you are aware, not all souls choose to pretend to separate themselves from this state of unity or oneness in order to experience the physical dimensions. For the purposes of our discussion, I will state that most souls do not make this choice. I apologize for my difficulty with the concepts of some and most, as I find it troublesome to communicate a concept that tries to enumerate souls. One is one. Any part of one is truly still one, therefore, most of one or some of one is artificial universally and I am a universal being, not an earthly being. I find great humor in your thought that perhaps I am just not good at math. It does not apply to me or to my work and I am perhaps making this harder than it need be. Let me begin again and comfort myself with the caveat that our discussion will be from an earthly perspective. This is a place of absolute truth and that place is not. The whole truth, as well as the truth of the whole, is masked or hidden in that place. I must try to remember that as we speak. Let us continue, please. Our topic of discussion began with soul groups. I will try harder to not digress so far from my point, but I appreciate that you are willing to listen to all that I try to say. Thank you.

Souls are all connected, both while in a physical dimension as well as when not so occupied. In essence, all that is learned by one is learned by all. The lessons learned during a visit to a physical lifetime aid in the expansion and evolution of all and that provides a valid reason to choose to incarnate. However, the primary reason that souls choose to incarnate is to experience the physicality of those dimensions where free will dominates the workings. Experiences are also shared among souls upon their return home, but as illogical as this may sound to you in consideration of your current situation, these lifetimes are greatly prized for the precise reasons that they are frustrating. The limitations within physical dimensions create an experience of sensation, emotion, and separation that are nearly impossible to replicate outside of the physical planes. The very same limitations possess the potential for the fastest and widest scope of evolution of the souls involved.

In the physical planes a soul has the opportunity to feel the most godlike that it can feel, illogical but true. Each and every experience, as well as each and every choice, exercises the creative abilities of a soul. In other planes free will is a minimal aspect of the experience and, thus, there is little or no opportunity to create or recreate, because there is no need. Outside of the physical planes, where nothing takes a material form, all of creation is shared and is expressed internally, so the individual experience of experimentation and the possibility of making mistakes are non-existent. Mistakes are joyous things and the resolution of mistakes is a glorious act that is generally the purview of the creator.

The physical worlds are truly lands of opportunity for a soul and the experiences gained there are treasured. For this reason, it is often the case that souls choose to return again and again to experience those places and souls very often choose to incarnate with other souls with which they have shared these experiences. Often this is done to balance energies between souls. Often it is undertaken to reverse roles in the making and correcting of mistakes. Often it is undertaken purely for the purpose of being incarnate once again. I am glad that you have learned from your teachers that the idea of a mistake is only an earthly property, so that you understand that there are not really mistakes, only different forms of experience and creativity; it has saved me from digressing once again.

Soul groups, as you also know from your teachers, are very flexible and fluid in nature. Souls join a group planning to incarnate and may stay with the core members of that group for many lives or they may choose another group on their next journey, so by definition a soul group forms for a single incarnation in most cases. The group formed includes not only the incarnating souls, but *also* all of the guides, angels, teachers, and masters of each soul. Some souls share teachers and guides. Some do not. It is quite a feat, really, for a soul to be so deeply involved in the illusion that it can feel alone among such a crowd, but that loneness is a valued part of the experience.

Singularity cannot be dreamt of, let alone experienced, within the unity of creation. Relationships, conflicts, and differences cannot be experienced within the unity of the universe. Darkness cannot be known from within the light of home. It is the very illusionary nature of the physical planes that attracts souls. The soul who longs for heaven while on earth will be the same soul who longs for earth while in heaven and each soul who so longs shares this longing with all others who have been brave enough to venture into a lifetime in the material.

I hear you asking for confirmation that souls incarnate into several lives concurrently and I will tell you that my best answer is yes and no. Each soul chooses this for itself. Often a soul incarnates into a physical plane while also incarnating into a nonphysical plane or incarnates and remains at home. All of these choices are a function of the nature of time, which exists only in the physical dimensions and not universally. All that exists operates both in the instant and in the eternal, as they are one and the same, but perhaps that subject is better left for another discussion.

Again, for now I wish you love and peace until we speak again.

Sarassa, August 14, 2012

Chapter Five

WE ARE NOT ALONE

I am here. I am your friend Rashka and I am happy to be with you. Let us talk of the other beings and energies with which you share the earth. It is a good question and I am glad to answer your questions, my friend.

Some of the nonhuman life forms on the earth are knowable to the eye and others are not as yet out of hiding. Those that could be seen have been seen by those with a gift of second sight. Some can be heard by those who hear what most do not. Some can only be felt and are but rarely recognized in their truth. We can and will discuss, as a part of this topic of instruction, the hidden nature of the beings of the natural world also, as they are not what they seem.

Among the residents and visitors of the earth plane are many representatives of other worlds and other dimensions who either serve or observe, generally unseen. Many clues exist to the presence of the others in song, art, and mythology, both ancient and current mythology, but are usually dismissed as being fictitious. Also among these beings are the guides, angels, and other servants of the earth and her inhabitants, both human and nonhuman. These are chief among those that can sometimes be heard and felt. It is a rarity for these beings to manifest a physical presence, but it can be done and has been done when this is the best method of care and guidance.

Also among the inhabitants of the earth are the representatives or remnants, if you will, of ancient ethereal cultures, who have chosen to remain with the planet in secret, hidden in nature and within the earth.

Most, if not all, of the beings of myth and fable also cohabitate in spirit or in physical form. Those who take form usually hide, but can be seen and heard by the curious and the believers. Look to your fables, fairy tales, and mythological tales for clues to these beings: fairies, trolls, gnomes, fauns, centaurs, giants, dragons, winged horses, and the like have their basis in fact and not in imagination. Many more humans than are willing to discuss these matters, lest they face ridicule, have encountered these beings.

I know that you are interested in the nature of the physical elementals and these will also be addressed as our discussions progress. Related to these elementals, but more complex, are the beings who create and maintain the physical workings of the earth. You have personal experience with the sentience of the earth plane, who infiltrates and encompasses that plane. Many assist her in her service, also, and were known as earth spirits, water spirits, and the deities of fire, air, and the animal and mineral kingdoms.

Again, we will tell you that we are amazed and entertained by the human notion of being alone, when there is such a multitude among you. Please allow us to continue these discussions, as I am sure that you can see that there is much to discuss. Until then, I am in your service in love.

Rashka, September 16, 2012

I am here. I am called by the name of Allinnana and we have not yet met. I am among your group of teachers and I appreciate your patience with me, as I have not communicated in this manner before and it took a moment to adjust. I bring with me the best wishes and love of your teacher Josiah, who speaks so fondly of you. We know that you have missed the aid of Josiah in your workings. He has been occupied of late in a course of instruction with new souls who prepare for their initial journeys into physical planes. There is need of additional instruction in light of the changes on the earth which reflect throughout all of the created universes. Josiah sends his best regards and looks forward to speaking with you again as soon as possible.

I have come to you in his stead to help to teach of the ways of the nature kingdoms because this is my area of expertise. I communicate, generally, with the members of the nature kingdoms and long, long ago it was the honor of my soul family to assist in the seeding of the earth.

It is coming to be known by more than a mere few among mankind that life extends beyond the human form in a conscious, intelligent manner. This is not new knowledge that is being sent to the earth, but is ancient knowledge that had been forgotten for a very long time and lived only in myth and legend. When the earth offered her self as a home and haven for life forms, those who came to the earth knew each other as sentient beings and the earth thrived with the great diversity of life forms in, upon, and near the planet. Each being, as it arrived, remembered the unity of all life. This was a grand time in the history of the planet as each new life or each new life form became a part of the planetary system in a cooperative manner. Each offered its service to the whole and added to the design until the planet teemed with life of all kinds. There was much experimentation and adjustment as the pieces of the puzzle combined to build a planetary system that was both beautiful and functional to the best ability of each life form.

This was the time of the mythological creation stories, which have altered over time, omitting the creativity of each type of life in favor of a design of creation that was directed from outside of the process. No such process would have been possible, my friend, simply because all that exists is alive and conscious and no material form can be created without the cooperation of its components. No form of life has the ability to create any physical or energetic material or form by sheer force. All that is created or altered in any manner is possible only with the cooperation of the energies or elements involved. This is as it should be. All beings in all forms, at the level of their souls or their divinity, are generous in their spirit of cooperation with one another. Withholding of love, acceptance, or permission is unnatural in the universe.

You can see, however, how, within a physical universe that operates within its own designed system of limitations and lack, the inherent diminished communication and awareness could create a false sense of disconnection among living beings that could empower the illusion that some are alive and cognizant while others are not. While very far from the truth of the nature of life, in such a physical world this illusion also serves a purpose. If it did not, it would not exist. All of life is both joyful and purposeful, and all of life, in love, cooperates to the best of its ability with all other life. Because in truth all life is one, it can be no other way. Even within a physical world, where there is diminished awareness, all life forms cooperate whenever possible toward a goal or purpose that benefits any part of life as though it was the whole of life, because in truth it is.

With this foundational explanation complete, let us move on to discuss some of the workings of the natural kingdoms. I did not feel that any discussion of this structure or organization would be easily understood without including the concept of cooperation and sense of purpose in the discussion. Thank you for your patience.

Any energetic being that chooses to alter its form in order to participate in a physical and material plane of existence retains, within the material structure, a connection to its perfect form. This is an important point within this discussion. Because this connection is maintained, all energetic and material form, regardless of size or complexity, is connected to its truth and to the truth of the unity of all life. All that exists, either materially or energetically, is alive and cognizant of its beingness. Were it not, it would not exist and non-existence is a false concept. There is no such thing as nothing. Any concept or system that contains an element or an idea of nothing is false.

Please do not equate false with bad. All of life is purposeful and it can serve a purpose to create a system that contains falsehoods. As with all things, each part of the whole contains the whole and the whole contains all of its parts. Therefore, anything that is false is a part of the truth and is connected to the truth. All that seems separate is connected to the whole. A falsehood is a clue or a path to truth. A part of the whole is a clue or a path to the whole. Each is, therefore, purposeful. Have I made this clear?

Each element of the natural world exists in its chosen form to serve the greater purpose of the whole of the world. Each world exists to serve the whole of existence. All such service is cooperative and informed. All that exists cooperates in each moment toward the highest and best purpose of all of existence. Life is not fixed, even though it is always balanced and stable. All of life is ever changing, growing, altering form and dimensionality. In each moment the totality of life is perfect in form and functions to suit and serve life's purpose. In each moment all is truly right with the world and with all of the worlds. In the next moment all will truly be right with the world, as its purpose exists in that moment, and each and all that the world contains will exist in form and function in perfect alignment with that moment's purpose. It can be no other way.

Let us please speak again.

Allinnana, September 22, 2012

I am here. I am your teacher Isahal. I am glad that you took the time to speak with me today. I also have information for you. Shall we begin?

There is much about the inhabitants of the earth that has been kept in secret through the times of density and darkness that has been upon the earth for many millennia. All through these dark times, there have been many beings among the residents of earth who served in secret.

Some are very ethereal in form and blended well into nature, showing themselves only rarely to those who were awakened, and some were representatives of other worlds who lived upon the planet or visited the planet in disguise. The secrecy of their presence was intentional so as not to interfere in the progress of the journey toward ascension. Some were much more observers of the doings of the human beings, while others were in place to assist and protect. Among the protectors were guides and angels in service to particular groups of incarnate souls, who maintained the ability to take material form as was necessary to deliver messages and assistance in times of crisis. Please know that their service and assistance was, for the most part, prearranged by the incarnate as a fail safe mechanism.

Those who served the planet, or a part of the planetary system, were serving a mission to aid a kingdom in particular and there are far more servants of the natural kingdoms upon the planet than there are servants of mankind. Those who serve the animal kingdoms are known by the species whom they serve, as they operate within the ranges of hearing, sound, and sight that are accessible to the animals, that are outside of the range of human senses, generally. These beings are sometimes known as animal spirits or totems. While they can take the form of an animal, they are, in fact, not animals. They are spirit beings that are closely connected to the animals of the planet.

It is the same for the spirits that serve the plant kingdoms, from the smallest organism to the largest. These guides and helpers also can take the form of the plants that they serve. They may be mistaken by man for a nature deva or a plant spirit. It is they who can communicate with members of the other kingdoms. Because plant species may spend only a short time on the planet, it is these plant guardians who hold much of the information needed by the plant kingdoms. Their voices or songs can be heard in the forest, the ocean, and the field, but they are rarely recognized outside of their kingdoms, except by healers and shamans who ask their advice and respect their presence and their service.

Also walking the earth, and in some cases living above and below the earth, are representatives of ancient civilizations who chose to stay with the planet when their civilizations left. Chief among these are the Lemurians, who stay out of love for the world. Their service is great to the world in healing damage and patiently holding ancient knowledge. As the vibrations continue to adjust upon the planet, many of these beings will be made visible upon the earth, as it will be time for their knowledge and wisdom to again be assured.

Isahal, September 24, 2012

I am here. I am glad to be with you again. May we continue?

We were discussing the presence of the unseen and the unknown in the earth plane. Please know that there are spirits also upon the earth from other ancient cultures and civilizations. There are representatives of many of the ancient indigenous cultures of the earth who have returned to be of assistance during this period of change. They also hold very valuable knowledge and technologies that they have begun to release and share in preparation for ascension. Please know that the advances in communication technologies have been released in the recent past as a means of opening the possibility of direct mass communications that serve to prepare for the return of communications between people and between kingdoms without the aid of machines and technologies. Can you understand how the change from a system of communication controlled by organizations of great power to a system freely accessible by all would first need to have the belief that such a system of open communication were possible? Such a system of unified communication has remained in the nonhuman kingdoms. It is gaining acceptance at a very rapid pace among the human kingdom and it will now be easier to accept this form of communication between and among all of the kingdoms as it is revealed in the changing vibrations of the planet.

It is not just this kind of service that has been provided in relation to ancient technologies by the hidden members of the ancient cultures of the earth. It is true that nothing that can be imagined cannot be created, and it follows that creation is always preceded by acceptance of the possibility or imagination of the outcome. I will explain that the word imagination refers to the image of an outcome being held and not the invention of a new idea or form. First the image and then the reality is created. The representatives of the ancient kingdoms have held the images and are releasing them into the physical plane so that they can then be made manifest once again.

As they begin to emerge from hiding, the unseen residents of the planet will once again be seen in forms related to their physical environments and their fields of service. In their chosen forms are clues to their service. Those beings who take form resembling animals will be known to be of service to the animal kingdom. Those who take hybrid forms, such as fairies, trolls, and the like, will be recognized as serving to bridge the kingdoms that their forms represent. For example, those creatures of myth and legend that evidence themselves with wings added to a human or animal form, or any combination of forms related to one or more of the nature kingdoms, will be known as representatives of heaven. Humans hold the belief that heaven exists separate from the earth and that it is located above the planet. It is only this commonly held belief that necessitates a means of flight from one to the other. There is no harm in this belief in winged denizens of heaven and, therefore, the presence of wings will only serve to ease the association of these beings with their divine service.

There is much more to discuss on this topic, but I suggest that another time will serve as well as the present for continuation of our discussion. I leave you in peace and love.

Isahal, September 25, 2012

I am here. I am your friend and teacher Isahal and I am glad to be with you again. I appreciate you taking the time to speak with me this day. Let us continue our discussion. We have been talking about the other beings on the planet. This day let us discuss the beings from other worlds that walk among the residents of the planet, if it pleases you.

For almost as long as the planet has existed in a material form, it has been both visited and aided by beings from other worlds and other dimensions. Please remember that that planet was formed for the purpose of providing an arena on which beings could experience existence within a physical environment, designed to accommodate the wishes of evolving souls to learn about themselves. This learning was accomplished by stepping into a dimension and a universe that was designed and built to limit or restrict the scope of experience in order to teach about the whole by experiencing only parts of the whole. Because of this design and purpose, only a part of the souls who chose to participate were involved within this environment. Were the entire soul involved and activated, the purpose of that *involvement* could not be fulfilled. At various stages of the planet's life there have been greater or lesser restrictions imposed, as suited the needs and desires of the incarnating souls, which resulted in cyclical periods of density and light. Throughout all of these cycles, the planet has been occupied by both the seen and the unseen in varying degrees.

The material and physical universe is not as it appears from within. Although it is designed to appear to be a collection of individual components, it is truly a living, growing organism that is ever changing in form and purpose. Because of its very nature, it could be correctly said that almost all of the inhabitants of a physical universe are alien; each transplanted or seeded from another aspect of creation.

For the purpose of our discussion, however, let us refer to the alien inhabitants and visitors to that physical universe as those beings who do not incarnate in a human form within and subject to the physical laws of that plane. This distinction being made, it should be understood that the form taken by alien visitors to that place often includes human forms so well adapted to the environment that they are indistinguishable from what we shall call human beings.

Most of the alien visitors that visit, unseen or disguised as nonhuman beings, visit to observe. They do not require a human form, or really any form at all, to observe. They visit to observe, not to be observed, and so, with the rare exception of being perceived by those gifted with the ability to perceive the unseen, their presence has always been secretive.

Those visitors who disguise themselves as human beings have, for the most part, been those who serve or assist the development of the cultures of the physical worlds by delivering clues, signs, and technologies to the physical worlds as needed for evolution of the masses, rather than assisting individual souls or soul groups that are incarnate in these worlds. It is true that it is often the contribution of these alien visitors that explains the introduction on a large scale of knowledge or technology that is justified by the evolution of a sufficient number of incarnate souls to allow for assistance with the uplifting of the rest to a comparable level. It is also true that the opposite point could be made that devolvement of a sufficient number of souls has been known to justify the introduction of technologies that serve to lower the level of the masses, as conditions or changes of purpose dictate, during a darker cycle upon the world.

In the current cycle, it has been decided to ascend the state of being of that physical universe as a whole and the knowledge and technologies being delivered at this time, as well as those delivered in the recent past, are of a different nature than those utilized in the past to adjust or alter cultures and civilizations. So it will be that the service of those who deliver this knowledge is also different than in the past and will allow for the exposure of the presence and purpose of many of these alien visitors. The recognition and acknowledgement of their purpose and presence serves unity and achievement of a fuller understanding of unity is driving the process of ascension.

Also among the inhabitants of the world, both seen and unseen, are the divine beings who serve souls and soul groups. These beings, by whatever names they have been assigned, arrived upon the planet with the first group of souls that chose to incarnate and will stay until the very last soul has left that plane. Look to the arts and legends, both ancient and recent, for evidence of their deeds and presence. Always able to take any form necessitated by their service, they have often been seen and heard. Yet, their presence remains the subject of debate and belief. This, too, will soon change as evidence of divinity also serves the lesson of unity that is key to the ongoing process of ascension.

Let us stop here for now, my friend.

Isahal, October 1, 2012

I am here. I am your friend, your brother, and your protector. I am so glad to be speaking with you once again. You have been discussing the unseen visitors to that plane with the teachers and it is a worthy topic. I would like to offer you information also. As you are aware, as a part of my service other than my favorite service, which is to you; I work with the energetic forces and grids. If you are interested, I would be pleased to share with you and your readers of my knowledge on this subject. Let us begin.

As the teachers have previously related, all that contains energy or energy in the form of matter is alive and has consciousness. The energetic forces active in the physical plane, therefore, constitute living beings and co-exist on that plane with the many life forms that are more easily recognizable as living beings. It is, in fact, the divine spark of life that contributes consciousness to the energetic workings and mechanisms of magnetic fields, electricity, gravity, and tectonics. Although each of these energetic systems is influenced by the sentience of the solar systems and the groups of souls who guide their adjustments and alter their workings, the energy forms themselves carry a massive consciousness of their own, which carefully maintains and monitors their status in alignment with their purpose.

You are correct in your thought that similarly the systems or sentience that manage and maintain other forces of nature, such as oceanic, atmospheric, and geologic systems are also nonhuman energetic beings unrecognized as such within the physical planes. You have knowledge of the evidence that water reacts to thoughts and expressions of gratitude and love. There is also abundant evidence of a similar reaction by members of the plant and animal kingdoms. All that I would add is that these measurable reactions are not, in fact, in response to thought, but are rather responses to the expression of emotion.

Emotion is a much more complete expression than thought. While thought carries its own unique energy signature or charge throughout the physical universe, its structure is temporary and changeable, and while thought can lead to the establishment of larger, more substantial energy structures, thought is still incomplete and not aligned fully with the unified state of the universe. It is, therefore, not the thought of gratitude that affects material structures, but the expression of the emotion of gratitude that is understood and acknowledged. All true and effective communication originates in the heart, not in the mind. Thought is related to illusion. Emotion is related to reality. It would be beneficial to apply this knowledge to the assessment of the value of information that is received and sent.

Remember that all that is of nature, energy, and the soul distinguishes truth from fallacy on this basis. The human will is based in the mind as it relates to man's interaction with others. Being based in thought, the structure of the will and its effect are also temporal and illusional, which befits the human experience in form and function. All interactions between the souls or the essences of living beings that are heart based result in true communication and lasting consequences. All that creates change is based in cooperative functions between and among energetic beings.

Exposure of your heart to the world and to the universe creates true communication and will be met in kind. Peace begets peace. Love begets love. Respect begets respect. Sadness will be comforted until it is love. All else is temporary and of the world only.

Serrale, October 11, 2012

Chapter Six

WISDOM OF THE ANCIENTS

I am here. I am called Laheenah. We have not spoken for a while and it is good to be with you again. Because you ask about my name, I will gladly explain its origins. My peoples are those of the island cultures whose descendents populate Polynesia, Indonesia, and other island cultures. My people are descendants of one of the peoples of the island civilization of Atlantis of long ago, many of whom traveled across the seas as the end of that civilization approached and chose a simpler culture that thrived in alignment with the planet. This brought us great peace and joy for many generations and we fared well until the world became darker and denser. These heavier conditions have caused our descendants difficulty, except for those who managed to stay as isolated as possible from the world outside of their own cultures. We are holding the joy within our last surviving cultures until it can be again released as the darkness lifts.

There are many myths about our ancient cultures that contain little or no truth, as these stories were told by others about us. We have never been warrior cultures and would never have participated in rituals of sacrifice, as we have always kept the understanding of the divine nature of all life. Thus, we know that life encourages and supports life and that death and war encourage and support death and war. This mythology created fear of our peoples, but did not create fear among our peoples. We wanted only to be left in peace for as long as possible.

Because we were island peoples, we learned much from the element of fire that creates islands and learned much from the seas that sustained life upon the islands. It is joyful to live in balance with that which holds land forms together and with that *which* exists in constant movement. We have always been happy and grateful people and each day brings forth cause for celebration for the gifts that the world bestows, and so it is joy that I wish to speak of this day. Contrary to how it may appear, your world is not lacking joy, only your lives are lacking joy. Joy exists in its own right as a natural force in great abundance. Like many natural forces in abundance upon that world, it only lacks recognition. It does not feel forgotten because so few see it in their lives. It feels only joy and is self-sustained in its existence.

Much like beauty, which is also a force of nature, joy lives in joy whether or not it is felt to exist. Beauty exists in beauty whether or not it is seen. Joy, beauty, peace, compassion, and love offer their gifts without regard to their acceptance, for each is pure in form and self-sustaining. Do you understand? Joy is not absent in any situation or location. As beauty is said to be in the eye of the beholder, it could also be said that joy is in the body of the grateful being. Joy encourages and engenders movement and expression. Joy dances and sings. Joy laughs and plays. When encountered and recognized, joy expands. When ignored, joy waits, for joy does not require a host, it only enjoys one. Joy is not manmade, joy is universal and, thus, it shares itself universally.

I am pleased to share with you the wisdom of the island peoples and am honored that you ask this of me. Let us continue. In times past, long ago, there were many peoples of the island continent. They had been seeded or sent from different worlds to that one, at each one's own request, to build a culture of unity among the human beings and the world. Because their intent was strong, their success was great and each and all learned from each other and cooperated to create much that was new and brilliant upon the earth, creations that would probably not have been possible upon the individual worlds from which the original beings came. Each such creation was honored and celebrated, but only those best suited to the vibrations of the earth were retained. This was a culture of cooperation that held very high light vibrations, so the conversion of energy to form or the changing of form was simple and elegant. For many more years than can easily be recalled, it was thus and the peoples of the island culture lived in harmony, peace, and joy. After a long time, however, the best and most creative of the people yearned for challenges from which to learn and expand their understanding of the workings of the material and physical planes. So it was that the changes in the energy vibrations in and of their place were brought forth and the light was dimmed, little by little, so that challenges arose in the creative process as planned.

There was still much joy with each new triumph and each new failure as the material characteristics became denser in reaction to the changes in the light. It is true that the density did not suit all beings among the people, and many who wished not to change form or focus during these transitions chose to depart. They left behind much of their wisdom and their origins within the civilization, for the benefit of those beings who remained. Being so short a time upon the earth, these ancient peoples returned to their light forms happily and *were* grateful for the knowledge that they had gained. Over much time, as the density increased according to plan, a point approached not unlike your own time, when the inevitable outcome of these gradual changes appeared on the horizon of the civilization. A choice approached to reverse the flow of energies from the material toward the light or to continue past a point of balance into density and darkness that would significantly affect the form and purpose of the civilization, past a veil of darkness and into your modern world. The structure of the island civilization soon became too dense to hold its original form as a consequence of this choice, and it was during this time that the remaining peoples of the island sought new beginnings on more solid ground.

The island continent was not lost. No energy form is ever lost. It changed as all things change. The ways and the wisdom of the island peoples were not lost. They became harder to see and remember in the deepening density, but survived in the knowledge of the souls involved in the creation. The old ways were not forgotten for a very long time. They just did not operate as they once did in a world whose properties had changed, and so they became mythology so that the resulting cultures could honor the old ways and pass the memories along until such time as the energies returned back over the balance point into the light and the old ways could again operate within yet another new world. All is as it should be. This threshold again approaches and it is with great joy that many of the original island peoples anticipate a return to that place.

For now, I leave you in love.

Laheenah, June 12, 2012

I am here. I am called by the name of Laheenah and I am glad to be speaking with you again, my dearest friend. Thank you for taking the time to speak with us. It is a joy for us to be in your space. When we last spoke, we were discussing the wisdom and the ways of the ancient island peoples. If we may, I would like to talk further on this subject. Thank you.

As you know, the ancient island peoples were a joyful people. If you remember, we also discussed the intimate connection between the people and their world. It is a renewal of this state of cooperation and intimacy between human occupants of the planet and the planet herself that will bear the most rapid ascension results as the energy changes of the new earth become established. It will then quickly follow this renewed state of harmony, that the connection and cooperation of all of the planet's inhabitants will be established. The planet herself will assist in this process, as much time has passed since mankind operated in a manner that encouraged trust in its relationships with the animal, plant, and mineral kingdoms, and the other kingdoms would be slow to trust humans without the example and the encouragement of the earth mother toward this goal. The nonhuman kingdoms operate, as you will remember, in a clearer state than mankind, but they all, as part of the divine essence of all of life, hold consciousness and purpose even while in physical form. They cooperate and communicate clearly within and between their kingdoms, as they have always done. It was the changes in purpose of the human kingdom that eventually led to a state of isolation from the unity of the planet's inhabitants. I know that you understand that there is no blame or shame in the changes that occurred; they simply suited the changes in the nature of the experience and lesson of the souls incarnate, but within the increased density that resulted from these changes the unity seemed to be lost. The elements of the earth still spoke to man, but he came to listen with his ears instead of his heart and he heard them no more. Receiving no reply to their songs and whispers, the elements eventually felt separate from mankind and this saddened them greatly. Few and fewer among men could hear and see the hearts of the elements of the world and soon the world found little joy in their interactions with mankind.

Mankind withheld its love from the world and came to forget the love of the past and the world was sadder still, and so it was that the world seemed to be a darker, sadder, and difficult place for souls to inhabit and the world reflected back to man the changed energies that he had designed, even though he did not remember being the creator of the darkness. Man came to view the earth as a foe and set out to force his will upon his world, directing his baser emotions upon his own reflection, which he no longer recognized as a part of himself, because he saw the world with his eyes and not with his heart.

Man could not see the plan in the darkness and the elemental kingdoms had learned to feel separate from mankind, but the sentience of the earth knew and remembered all within her care and knows the truth and the dreams of all souls upon the world. In a world changed to reflect judgment, opposition, exclusion, and conditional love and acceptance, the earth mother held truth and love in its pure form. She holds it always available for the asking. Herein lies the key to the first step of ascension. Many who walk the path toward heaven on earth will recall the moment of renewed communion with the earth mother as an experience of transcendence or as a moment of pure love and joy that altered the course of their life journey. You know this to be true.

And so, I now ask you to listen carefully to the second step on the path of ascension. Do not slip back upon the labored path of life for too long a time. It is worthy to examine your path through eyes that have seen transcendence for the sake of the lesson this contains, but do not tarry long on this task. Return to the light and love of the earth mother's gift and hold it unto your heart. Her love knows no bounds and it will flow to you in each moment, if you will but remember to ask. In the light of her love shall all that was veiled from your heart be restored. Her love will guide and protect you as our love guides and protects you. It can be no other way, for her love is great in your service.

Laheenah, June 30, 2012

I am here. I am your friend and guide Rashka and I am at your service this and all days. Let us speak again of the wisdom of the lost civilizations as I know this is both of interest to you and relevant to the new earth to come. As you know, I was once a part of the peoples who populated Egypt in the times of its greatest glory. There is much to be learned about and from this ancient culture that has been silent for many years. As with most of the ancient civilizations and cultures, keys and clues to our knowledge have remained that the memory of their ways could be rekindled at this important time of change in the history of man and the earth. Please know that there is no accident in the artifacts and structures that have remained, both hidden awaiting rediscovery and in plain sight. These are but seeds left upon the earth with the purpose of holding the information they contain and standing as a doorway, of sorts, to the consciousness of the cultures that constructed them. These structures, writings, and markers have not remained by accident, but rather by grace, for they were intended as much for this time as for the time of their creation and have been kept safe.

Let us now speak of the study of history, as your thoughts lead us to an important topic. As the world begins to adjust to the energetic changes that lead into the new earth, there will be many aspects of the old earth that are being left behind because their energy signatures no longer are in harmony or agreement with the new energies.

The study of modern history is one such field of study that is losing its purpose in the approaching new earth. As the fourth and fifth dimensions are overlain upon the physical dimensions, concepts of time and space are altered and, as a result, it shall soon be common knowledge that the past and the future are, in fact, one with the present. The progress of the unification of the dimensional changes will be evidenced by the loss of interest and focus upon both the past and the future. These signs of change are evident and will be increasingly evident from this time forward. It may seem that the lessons of the past are being lost or disregarded by individuals and by societies, and this is, in fact, the case. The new earth that is being constructed as we speak, piece by piece, will bear such a small resemblance to the earth of the recent past that no comparison of the two will hold any relevance or value.

The study of ancient cultures bears much more relevance at this point along the path of change, but it too shall be of little value as the changes near completion. As the doors to the ancient ways and the ancient knowledge, that will assist the changes and the adaptations to the changes, are opened and absorbed into the new culture of the new earth, the keys and clues left by the ancient ones shall no longer serve and will no longer require safekeeping, as no key is required for an open door.

The clues left behind by the ancient ones were designed by cultures that held a much broader world view than those of earth's modern civilizations, and these cultures were much more unified across both time and space. This allowed for a purposeful design of the ancient keys embedded upon and within the earth for your use within the current period of change, therefore, it will soon be seen that the examination of the keys as a whole, rather than the examination of these cultures separately, is critical to understanding.

Many, but far from all, of the ancient cultures and civilizations were linked or joined within the lost civilizations of Lemuria and Atlantis. Others were much more ancient and others yet were from outside of the earth altogether, and yet, because time and space are only an illusion, they were all unified and all cooperated toward the growth and evolution of the earth and her inhabitants.

It may seem that much of what was in the past will be again in the future, but this philosophy is directly influenced by the effect of the illusion of time. In fact, all that was in the past as well as what will be in the future are one and the same in the present. The present is all that there truly is. Both the past and the future are illusions and this fact is the only connection that they share. I know that this is a concept that may seem difficult to grasp at first, but bears repeating, I think. It is only the illusion of the past that seems to bear any influence upon the illusion of the future.

Let us continue this discussion soon. For now, I leave you to rest and send peace and love.

Rashka, July 5, 2012

I am here. I am glad to speak with you again my friend. I am your teacher Isahal. I know that you have many questions for me and so it is good to be speaking with you again. Let us discuss more of the ancient cultures, as I have information on this topic, also, to share.

I would like to discuss the ancient cultures of the southern hemispheres, those that are now called aboriginal cultures. In times long ago upon the earth, there were several seed races, or cultures, and beings that originated from a physical universe outside of the one that contains that planet. Earth was, and remains, a grand experiment in creation and many different civilizations and beings joined the experiment in times long ago. Some of the ideas and creations that were adapted and brought forth upon the earth were quite successful and traces of them remain to this day. Many were successful for a time, but served out the purpose for which they were created and no vestiges of their existence remain. Many did not serve and were quickly withdrawn. It is quite entertaining, really, that the argument exists among men as to whether or not humans are alone in the universe and vast searches are conducted by scientists and warriors alike for proof of life on other planets, when they still do not see the other life on their own planet; very entertaining indeed.

Among the most successful adapted form of human to be introduced onto the earth were the people whose descendants are called aboriginal. At times, tribes or civilizations of these people occupied the vast majority of the southern hemisphere of the planet, which in times long ago was the most temperate in climate and was lush with plant life. Because the earth was abundant with all that was necessary for survival, these cultures could develop both technically and spiritually at a more rapid pace than others of the seed races that chose more formidable locations and lifestyles.

At the peak of their civilizations, which lasted many millennia; these cultures thrived in complete cooperation with their environments and communicated easily and fully with their sources, both their divine source and their physical source race. This ability allowed them to adjust or evolve quickly and easily to physical changes in their planetary environments and to adjust quickly and easily to new technology as the energetic systems of the planetary system changed over time.

Their knowledge of the structure of their universe was great, as was their knowledge of the mineral, plant, and energetic kingdoms with whom they coexisted. They brought from their home universe the ability to coexist in the physical and the nonphysical worlds and knew and trusted the dream worlds. They also knew and trusted the other physical kingdoms and lived in a state of harmony and open communication with their world. As a result, they served the world and the universe well and the world and the universe served them well in return. Each contributed freely to the needs and desires of the other and their world resembled the paradise of mythology, although their cultures have been much changed by the influence of other cultures and by the energetic changes of the earth system over time. They survive still with much of their cultural wisdom intact, kept in secret from a world that has become darker and more hostile, but kept alive awaiting the return of paradise. They hold in their songs, stories, and hearts the knowledge of the old ways of trust. They hold the truth of the nature of their world and they hold the secrets of communication and cooperation that once moved mountains, rivers, and seas and changed deserts to forests and back again.

These peoples remained, until the most modern of times, small in stature because they were enemies of none and had no need of large bodies for defense. Their small size created less of a burden upon their environment. As other races grew larger and more aggressive, they came to isolate themselves and carried on their cultures in relative peace. Even in modern times they were quite protected by their isolation and were viewed by modern man as children because of their small size and simple lifestyles. Contrary to the cultural assumptions of modern man, these are perhaps the most powerful human beings that have ever inhabited the earth. They hold vast knowledge within the wisdom of their silence. They understand the workings of the universe in ways both large and small. They have outlasted many civilizations and cultures that once thrived, if only briefly, upon the earth. Their earthly home is dear to them and they are dear to the earth. That, truly, is the definition of success for a human species, to respect and to be held in respect by the world you occupy. It also contains the key to survival of any race of being during times of change.

Let us speak later, my friend.

Isahal, July 14, 2012

I am here. I am called Isahal the Teacher and I am glad to be with you again, my friend. We have been discussing the ancient civilizations and I would like to continue, if we may. As we have previously discussed, there was much wisdom and power contained within the ancient cultures of the southern hemisphere. Many of these cultures predated the lost continent, but some are descendants of Atlantis. It was known for a very long time that the Atlantean continent would meet its end, as its purpose had been fulfilled and so it was during a period of change, not unlike the present time, that the continent was removed from the surface of the earth.

Much like your own time, many of its inhabitants participated in the coming changes and many did not believe that the plan would come to completion. Many of those who believed and listened to the planet as the change neared left the island continent for safer places. Only those who clung blindly to their own dogma were lost with the continent.

As you know, no soul is ever lost, but many suffered unnecessary damage during the transition. I do not refer to physical damage, of course, but rather spiritual damage was done because the disparity of their beliefs and the truth of the physical events confused these souls and they were, for quite a period, lost in their own disbelief. I relate this story to you only because it is the basis for the decision that during the next great period of change, the coming of the next age of the earth, that is now upon the planet, that all souls will be included in the change. It was the memories of the souls who once lived through the end times of Atlantis that requested a gentler change.

The previous changes that had accompanied the dawning of new ages of the earth had been fast and cataclysmic in nature. It was originally planned that it would also be so for the beginning of this new cycle of the earth. Your mythology and your major and minor religions had prophesied the change to be as of the times of old. It was the earnest request of the Atlanteans that was heard and it was their lesson that was learned and accepted, and so it was decided that this change could and would be reinvented as a more gentle and slower period of transition. It was a good and loving decision well made and it will be lovingly executed with the smoothest rate of physical change as possible, so that there is the least possible chance of damage to souls.

This does not mean that many souls who plan to depart the earth will not do so. This is a part of their planned life experience and they suffer no harm; they only chose to return home during the change, as the experience that they planned was focused on their participation at the beginning of the cycle and their service is completed as they return home in honor and grace. It was the welfare of the participants who are asleep, or as yet unaware of the coming changes, for whom the dispensation was made, and it has been done. Worry not for their souls. They will be tended to and their way will be eased and guided. It is truly befitting the entry of an age of peace that the end of the old age also be peaceful.

Let us speak again soon, my friend. I leave you in love for now.

Isahal, July 28, 2012

I am here. I am your teacher Isahal and I am again pleased to be in your presence. We still have much to discuss and so I thank you for inviting this conversation. I am pleased to teach. It is essential to my purpose and it gives me great pleasure.

If we may, let us continue our discussions of the wisdom of the earth's ancient peoples and cultures. There are still great stores of wisdom and nature based technologies contained within the traditions and ancient stories of the indigenous cultures of the world. These are seeds of rebirth of these forgotten, or perhaps better described as underappreciated, cultures. Look to the peoples who seem tied to the land as though it is a part of their family or a part of their cultural identity for the wisdom that will be needed in the new age of the earth. Please do not make exception for forced relocations of cultures. You will find among them a love of their home lands or their ancestral lands that is at least as strong as their connection to their adopted homes.

Underlying this love of a home land is a connection to the planet herself that is not held or understood by more modern cultures. Ancient cultures do not relocate for advancement. Modern cultures, or nomadic cultures, do not understand the power of an affiliation with the land of their people. Ancient peoples preserve the lands. Modern peoples exploit the lands. The lands can accept either of these conditions and survive, but it should be contemplated whether or not a culture or a people can tolerate either of these approaches as well and still survive.

The planet is designed to serve the life that she contains and fosters. She provides all that is necessary for the asking. The ancient cultures lived in grace upon the earth. They treated the planet with honor and respect and lived in gratitude. The planet responded with honor and respect and expressed her love for her children and her charges. There was trust felt and expressed between the planet and the peoples.

Civilizations developed that were darker in nature. This trust was forgotten and the people of the modern cultures did not carry the faith that their needs would always be met, and so they changed the relationship with their planet. They no longer asked for grace. They no longer felt gratitude. They were afraid of lack and so they hoarded and stole resources from others. As the modern cultures met the ancient cultures, the outcome was really quite predictable. The new people took from the older cultures, which were willing to share, until they had no more resources and still the new cultures demanded more. The new cultures took from the old their rituals and ravaged their sacred sites. The new cultures carried off markers and tools from their native locations that would be of no use to them in another site.

The people of the ancient cultures grieved these losses greatly and many descendants of the invaded cultures still await the return of the stolen artifacts to their proper homes. Many of the conquered peoples were so broken hearted that they chose to return home. They did not necessarily succumb to foreign disease, as it is believed, but rather chose their departure because without the home lands of which they were a part, too much of their identity was missing to sustain them. In many instances, a few brave souls stayed behind to hold and pass on the wisdom. Many went into hiding to keep safe their knowledge and their sense of cultural identity. Many of their stories and prophesies reflect this state of waiting for the return of the old ways to a new world or a new time, and there is much truth in these tales.

Slowly, their cultures have been regaining the respect of the past. It has been a long wait and their service and sacrifice has been great in this endeavor. Their service has been, and will be, crucial to the building of the new earth. All who have waited in hiding shall soon be rejoined and the effects of the combination of the individual pieces of wisdom and technology so long kept safe in secret then shall be truly marvelous to witness. So much that is ancient shall seem new. With the return of the ancient wisdom shall come a renewed faith and trust that shall soon restore heaven to earth. It is true. All of life cycles: changing and yet remaining the same. Each cycle, or wheel, turns, bringing gifts and trials. It is the way of the world, and so it is.

Isahal, August 9, 2012

Chapter Seven

WISDOM OF A GENERAL NATURE

Chapter Seven contains teachings on a variety of topics of general interest. Some information was sent to satisfy my curiosity or to provide answers to questions asked at the request of others.

ALTERNATE REALITIES

I am here. I am called Rashka. I am your friend and guide. I am so happy to be with you once again. Thank you for speaking with us this day. There is much to be discussed. May be begin?

We know that you have concerns about the information received from the eagle woman.

My friend, White Eagle, had relayed a premonition that she had received about an upcoming human caused disaster. She has the gift of communication with the animal kingdom. She had been told that she would be called to establish a sanctuary for animals and children, and was preparing for such.

She is a fine friend to the animal kingdom and we are glad that you are able to give her support in her work, which can seem a lonely path for her. She is a gifted soul and is much loved and well protected, especially by the animal spirits. She has received news of troubles and has been told to prepare. This message is a truth for her, but not necessarily for you. I know that his can be difficult to understand. Let me try to explain.

As the changes unfold, there will be created many intersections of dimensions, portals, and gateways upon the earth. Within these structures of energies there will exist many alternate realities much as exist outside of that plane. Alternate realities are alternate choice points, as such. As you are aware, the return of heaven to earth, while it could be overlain in an instant, will, in all probability, be instead a process. This choice of manifesting the energetic changes in stages is intentionally chosen because of the wide variances in the states of awakening, or enlightenment, of the planet's inhabitants. I say that this process is still a probability, because either enlightenment will be rapid or resisted, dependent upon the free will of all souls involved.

The end result is absolutely assured. It is only the process that still lies undetermined. It will be as it will be. The best interests and wishes of all will be honored. This is rightfully so. Because the path is still being walked, many different situations, or realities, have been designed to accommodate all who travel upon this journey. The roles of the enlightened will be also dependent upon their gifts and their paths.

Although much consideration was given to the creation of other physical worlds for the benefit of those who remain in deeper slumber, and, consequently there have been prophesies in the past of these other earths, it was ultimately decided to retain unity of souls during the dawn of the age. It was decided that none would ascend unless all ascended, and any designs for separate worlds were discarded long ago. Only the myth of this division of unenlightened from enlightened remains. This myth is the basis for the search for other worlds beyond earth to colonize and *this search* is now fruitless expenditure of resources based in false assumptions that spring from elitist dogma related to separation and competition for survival.

The first law of the new age of the new earth is unity. You correctly remember the phrase "all for one and one for all"; very good. No soul shall be lifted up at a pace that is faster than its choosing and this is why the alternate probabilities have been created. In the end there will again be only one truth for all, but none shall be forced or hurried along the path.

We will speak of this again soon. We wanted you to understand that there shall be many routes to the final destination and each will contain its own attributes as necessary for those who travel that way. All paths are honored. All will find their own way according to their needs and beliefs. No soul can ever be loved less than another. Each will be guided and protected. Be at peace with the knowledge of this, Beloved.

Rashka, December 30, 2011

CREATION

I am here. I came into your presence this day, with the assistance of your friend and guide Rashka, to answer your questions. I am honored to be in your space. I am called Laheenah and I am a representative of the circle of feminine energy keepers. I am aware that I am new to your communication circle. It is wise of you to check with your guide, as you have just done, but I suspect that you felt no harm in my vibration.

As you are always curious about your friends and their stories and origins, I will be happy to discuss these with you as they relate to my circle of energy workers or, perhaps better said, my circle of companions of the feminine energies. We are a group consisting of many souls who were born within and are attuned with the feminine aspect of the creative energies. While it is very true that the energies of creation are whole and balanced, they also contain, in perfect integration, aspects that could be defined as masculine, feminine, and neuter. Although all exist in cooperation and unity, each of these aspects, much like the different aspects of a personality, have an affinity or a preference for certain of the states and acts of creation and are, of course, free to serve where they are the most happy and fulfilled.

As you have suspected, the energies of creation share a range of purposes that include the creation of change, the maintenance of the status or stability after change, and the examination and analysis of the state of creation that often leads to a need for change once again. Therefore, the process of creation exists in a circular form. We who assist and serve the process of creation also are a circle of souls and sentiences in harmony with our purposes.

We are both a multitude and are a single force, as are all that exist; thus, I speak to you as a representative. Do you understand? Good.

Creation is both a process and a state of being and the two are not separate one from the other. Much as a creative idea lives in its nonphysical form as well as in the physical process at work while being creative, it also lives in the resulting manifestation of the creative thought form. It then awaits the change that will inevitably arise and give birth to a new version of its creation, and the cycle repeats. It is the natural way of the living process of creativity and creation alike.

The feminine, or nurturing, aspect of creation flourishes within the state of change that brings the new into existence. The masculine aspect of creation prefers to hold the creation in place as it accustoms itself to its new state. It is the work of the neutral aspect of creation to examine creation and to assess the relationship between its form and its purpose, not in judgment, but only as a reflection of the creativity or the creation. You can surely see how each of these aspects of creation serves the creative process while still being unified in purpose.

There are nuances and shades within the process of creation that we will gladly discuss in the future, but I have come this day to offer to you not only information, but also encouragement during these times of change. We ask that you and your brethren step as far as is comfortable for you into your own creativity. So much more will be possible as the light increases within that plane, and the best mechanism for adjusting to the change is to embrace it and join in the process as consciously as possible. This will make the changes gifts and not burdens. Be at peace and embrace the change. It will embrace you back.

Until we speak again, I send you love, light, and creativity.

Laheenah, January 21, 2012

CROP CIRCLES

I am here. I am your friend Isahal. I am glad that you have chosen to speak with us this day. You have many questions. Let us choose a topic and begin.

The circles in the crops, sands, and snows are intentionally created. Those that are manmade number but a few among the many, but cause an inordinate amount of confusion about the origins of these designs in relation to their number. We would ask that the hoaxed circles be ignored.

Identification of the manmade designs is very simple, as they include damaged crops and do not register the electromagnetic patterns of the true circles or designs. Location of the designs can also provide clues as to their authenticity. Were the locations of designs mapped, the manmade designs would appear as outliers among the geometric pattern as a whole. This is a function of the lack of understanding of the nature and purpose of a circle or design as a marker of an energy matrix and as an indicator of the strength and purpose of a particular location within the energetic grid.

Through the placement of these designs upon the earth, the energy grids are, in fact, attempting to communicate lost or forgotten information systems. The language of the symbols has yet to be deciphered by humanity. May I pose the possibility that the purpose is not necessarily for the use of humanity, but rather for other kingdoms? Although benefit could surely be gained by humanity through understanding of the information contained within the essence of the designs and understanding of the significance of their locations, it is surely true, at this time, that humanity is not the object of these communications at the present time. Were they intended as a direct communication with humanity, they would not be so mysterious.

The workings of the universe are much simpler than man imagines. There has never been, and will never be, any reason for cloaking the intentions of the divine in mystery. Even though we understand that humans dearly love mysteries, please be assured that the mysterious is the way of man, not the way of All That Is. And so it is, that was All That Is trying to communicate with humanity, a much more direct communication would occur. Humanity does not, as a general rule, appreciate nor even notice patterns of beauty within the natural world. As such, the placement of information within beautiful, complex patterns within the plant and mineral kingdoms would not logically be intended for humanity. Nature, on the other hand, is based in complex displays of beautiful patterns. These designs and circles are made of, and made for, the kingdoms of the natural world, which will not be misled from their purpose by forgeries.

For those humans who find interest in these designs, we will note that there is information of value contained in the locations of the true circles, as well as information related to the frequency of their occurrence, that is indicative of periods of change in the electromagnetic grids that overlay the surface of the planet, but the core instructions contained within these energetic designs are for the use of the nature kingdoms.

Isahal, January 8, 2012

GOD, THE CREATOR, ALL THAT IS

I am here. I am called Sarassa and I am glad to be with you again. You thought of me earlier today and I am responding to your loving thoughts. Thoughts of love are a powerful tool to communicate with your divine guides and angels, as we all speak the language of love. You have questions about god and the creator and this is a question worthy of an answer. I am certain that only a few have taken the time to consider that there may be more than expected around this topic and I am glad to answer.

It is a commonly held belief among most of the religions of that world that god, either as a father figure or as a combination of a god and goddess as mother and father figures, are omnipotent heads of a hierarchy of angels, masters, saints, and the like with god sitting above all divine and earthly beings in judgment and in grace. Most of these religions also assign the role of creator to this god figure, whose presence helps to explain those parts and mechanisms of heaven and earth that defy the logic of the human mind. Others of the world's religions divide the aspects of this god into some or many aspects, therefore creating many gods and goddesses with many forms and functions. The purpose of these multiple gods serve the same as the monotheistic religion's father or grandfather god, which is to explain the divine workings of the earth and the heavens in earthly terms. There is a valid point to be made here that the creation of the god or these gods served to connect the members of these religions with divinity on a level that allowed for a belief in the divine, even if in a limited form befitting the circumstances of the earth plane itself. In this way, god was created in the image of man, which made god more accessible to man.

In a monotheistic religion, god and the creator were one and the same. In religious orders that held multiple manifestations or aspects of god as separate deities, there was a creator in its own right. All served to explain the existence of life as intentional, purposeful, and limited, as a human mind that operates within a system of applied logic requires an explanation of the beginnings of something from seemingly nothing. *This* was appropriate within the context of a physical plane where the majority of existence was hidden from view. A god or gods separate from mankind is only needed in a place of separation and so this became a truth of that place. Thoughts create what is, and so it was that the belief in a god, a creator, or a group of gods caused each to be.

All That Is, however, is not a god. All That Is exists, has always existed, and will always exist as the unified form of all that lives. All That Is is complex, but All That Is is not complicated. All That Is is large beyond comprehension of the human mind. All That Is knows all of itself in each moment. All That Is is one being. All That Is is without beginning and without end.

Sarassa, September 19, 2012

HARMONICS

I am here. I am called Isahal. It is good to speak with you again. I am glad to answer your questions. I am also a teacher, as is your friend Josiah. I am glad to be able to share information with you in this way. We who teach are engaged in instruction on this side of the veil for those souls who wish to learn and understand while not physically incarnate, as well as teaching in this manner, and others, with souls who are incarnate. Please understand that we learn as much as we teach through contacts such as these. It is an honor to be trusted with your life experiences, they teach us much. As I have always been a teacher or a student, I have not been born into the physical plane. I am, therefore, as curious about the workings of such places as those who seek knowledge of home.

You have many questions. If it pleases you, I will choose the topic for our discussion this day. Let us speak of harmonics. There will be a very important role in the new earth for sound, and so much information about its function and use has been forgotten in that plane.

Harmonics is the science of sound and tone. Although its remnants remain in the study of music, the vast majority of its properties are no longer understood on earth. Harmonics will once again be utilized on the new earth for communication, healing, and mechanical purposes, as well as for musical works. It would be advantageous to understand the basic workings of harmonics as it once was used, as well as its potential in the near future. Harmonics differs from sound, as you are aware. Although there are, and have been, efforts to use sound in the third dimensional earth plane for healing and medical diagnoses and, of course, for weapon design, these attempts to utilize sound are at best primitive compared to the potential of harmonics. Again, the limitations have derived from the third dimensional assumptions about separation. Because it has been believed that purpose can be obtained from sound by isolating certain tones of sound and then amplifying these isolated tones, the imperfect results reflect the imperfect understanding of the nature of sound.

The full beauty and the full force of sound can only be achieved by the use of combinations, or families, of sound. Sound is like much else within the physical planes, in that only a small part of the whole of sound can be detected, measured, and reproduced within the limitations in place in the physical planes. While many are aware that there are sounds utilized by many species within the nature kingdoms, little has been studied about these hidden frequencies, in part because mankind holds itself separate from the nature kingdoms and in part because of the reliance upon instrumentation in scientific study. Does it not seem odd that the clue within the language has been missed; that being that the word instrument refers to a tool used in medicine, a tool used in manufacturing, a device used in measurement, and an object that produces music?

The use of harmonics will again resurface on the new earth when a more complete understanding is regained of the vastness of the range of sound. When this remembrance, combined with the universal laws of mathematics, in particular sacred geometry, is applied to sound *it will* once again create the combinations of tones necessary to utilize harmonics. There is much power contained within the combinations of tones for communication within and between the kingdoms. Clues were left within music. Clues were left within mathematics. When the artificial barriers are crossed between art and science, much will be gained that will yet prove to be a valuable resource for good in that place. It will find itself among many new sources of energy that do not deplete the earth. You shall see.

I am glad to have been with you once again. Until we speak again, remember that you are loved.

Isahal, December 6, 2011

LANGUAGE

I am here. I am called Isahal and I am a teacher. I am glad to be in your presence once again. If I may choose the topic of this day's discussion, I would like to speak to you of language. Let us begin.

Language is widely used in the physical planes as a form of communication. This was not always so, and its use varies greatly dependent upon the purpose and structure of the world in which it is used. Within civilizations or worlds that are lighter in density, language finds itself of less usefulness than it does in denser worlds and civilizations. Language is of very little use outside of physical planes, except for cases such as these where communication is performed between dimensions, because so much experience is lost when translated into language from the more commonly used forms of telepathic, musical, and experiential forms of communication in general use throughout the universe.

There are many among the physical worlds that rely less on language, also. Where it is used in many other worlds, the cultures and civilizations are much more homogeneous than on your planet and there is little or no use for more than one language. Because the illusion of separation from source is one of the key elements in the structure of the stage of your planet, more opportunities for creation of factors of differentiation between human and source, human and nature, and human and human were created. These opportunities included race, gender, age, religion, and language. Each opportunity was created not as a piece of reality, but rather as a learning opportunity to be encountered, experienced, understood, and accepted or dismissed, as it befits the path of each soul upon that planet. Much emotion has been expended around these areas of separation, but this was not the original intent of their design and creation. They were designed as points of comparison and reflection, and in more enlightened periods they serve their original purpose well. However, in darker and denser times they tend to become points of contrast and conflict, and also serve their purpose well. The important part of learning is the journey through the lesson to the knowledge or realization at the end. The inherent ease or difficulty of the lesson is of little or no matter in the long run.

Always within the elements of separation created in a physical world, such as yours, are hidden markers and clues to the truth of their purpose. Hidden within the process of aging and the emotions associated with this process are clues to the truth of life, birth, and rebirth disguised within a process of deterioration and death. Hidden among the physical manifestations of racial differences are clues to the unity of purpose and commonality of experience. Hidden among the varying practices and dogma of religion are clues to the universal truths of hope and faith. Each form of separation and trial contains codes and keys to conquering the obstacles each presents, so that the treasures hidden therein might be exposed, freeing each soul to complete that cycle of learning and begin the next.

Within the structures of the languages of the earth are also encoded clues of assistance to the journeying souls. It is of particular note that the various languages of use in that place are also familial. For the most part, outside of languages purposefully designed for technical or machine use, the languages descend from another language, or family of languages, that have spread far upon the lands. Their origins, however, lead the speaker back to an ancestral land or people from whom the speaker, much like the language itself, has descended over the course of many lives. In times long ago, before language was necessary because of separation of families, clans, and the like, languages both spoken and written were of no use between peoples who still held their connections to their ancestors and their sources. In these times, memories and experiences were easily accessed both in the dream state and the waking state. Groups of people were much more aware of their common origins and were much more cooperative in relation to their common experiences and purpose.

In other physical worlds this is still the case, as most lifetimes in these worlds are structured and guided by divine means. It once was so upon your world, also, before the introduction of free will into the design and structure of that plane. Until there was individual choice of the methods and means of lifetimes in that world, there was no differentiation between "I" and "we".

With the arising of an "I" being, peoples came to believe that they were different one from another and came to design systems and languages that separated the "I" from the "we" of the past, and most of the connections between them came to fade in their memories. As the connections faded across time and distances, many of the collective memories of the people, along the way, also began to fade and came to be held solely by the shaman and the healer, who still bridged between the old ways and the new.

Soon it became necessary that language be written so that the old ways could be relearned across generations, because the generations spread across the lands and lost their connection to their families and their clansmen. The mythology of the invention of written language as an offshoot of commerce and law carries no truth. Its invention was designed to supplement the maintenance of the old ways and the old truths that were subject to misinterpretation in art and oral traditions. Safekeeping of the core truths of human origin and inter-dimensional existence were the sole purpose for the invention of language in general and the written language in particular.

While much of the experience of the old ways was lost within the use of language, as there is so much that cannot be transferred through words, the keys remained intact and still do. Those who study the ancient texts that were so faithfully and meticulously copied through countless generations can still find the seeds of truth living within the beliefs, stories, and rituals of the past, where they rest still awaiting fertile soil in which to sprout and bloom.

For now, my friend, let us part in anticipation of our next meeting. Remember that the teachers await your call, always.

Isahal, May 5, 2012

MAGNETICS AND MOTHER EARTH

I am here. I am your friend and guide Rashka and I came into your presence this day to inform and to comfort, as always.

Let us discuss the workings of the magnetic grids upon and within the planet, that are called by the name of ley lines, among others. As your mother planet is a living organism of great strength and longevity, she has helped to design and maintain a planetary body that holds life, contains life, and fosters life in a material plane.

It is very important to the workings of this planetary body that this chosen form be stable over time, but also capable of changes required to allow for changes within, and evolution of, the many species of life that she fosters. You are correct that there is a sort of correlation to the physical bodies maintained by the human, animal, and plant kingdoms that inhabit the planet, but the complexity of the planet's physical system far surpasses that of the kingdoms it contains. Her system acts upon, and interacts with, all forms of life beneath, upon, and above her planetary body and her sentience honors and serves each individually and all as a whole, for each and all are a part of her. Her influence reaches far beyond her surface and surrounding ethers into all corners of the physical universe of which she is a part and encompasses all within this universe and also interacts with all unseen within and without this physical universe.

We have discussed previously that the natural service of more feminine energies, as no energy form is only feminine, masculine, or neutral, to create change. Because this is true, it is only natural that she has always been felt as a mother, a nurturer, and a creative force. Her energies permeate all life within her physical universe in constant communication with the energies of the divine within all that exists in the physical and outside of the physical, in order that she might serve the highest and best purpose of all of life. All that she does is done in love and respect, because her soul is also made of love. The human attributes often ascribed to her are manmade. She is incapable of anger or revenge. Part of her service, in fact, is to absorb and cleanse such negative emotions, and she retains none of these *negative emotions* herself.

Among the tools contained within her physical system are magnetic grids and lines, not only within and upon the planet, but extending to the farthest reaches of the physical universe and beyond. These magnetic structures serve not only as an informational conduit, but also as an agent of cohesion within all that exists in a physical universe. They connect and support all physical manifestations as well as being a mechanical structure. These grids and lines not only convey information along their routes and within their structures, but they also contain information, knowledge, and wisdom of their own, as they are living forces that act upon the material and interact with the divine.

In times long past, man knew much more of the nature of these magnetics, as they were able to feel their presence and recognize their location and movement. Very ancient peoples were able to act in cooperation with the forces and structures of the natural world and also held their purpose and wisdom in esteem. The ancient legends and civilizations alike behaved *within* and conveyed the familial relationship between all of nature. They knew all of life to be connected as a family unit and lived in a state of cooperation and respect with their world. This was long and longer ago, but a seed of this truth still lives on in all that comprise and inhabit the planetary system, and shall yet burst forth from seed as the changing conditions shall soon allow. Remembrance of the true essence of the magnetic systems of the physical universe is the philosopher's stone of legend.

Until we speak again, I am your friend and sister.

Rashka, April 29, 2012

SASQUATCH

I am here. I am your friend and teacher Isahal. You have much on your mind today. It would be fun to discuss some of the topics that leave you puzzled. Do you agree? Let us begin.

You are curious about the beings that inhabit the planet for which proof is sought. I know of this. Like much that exists in that place that is usually unseen, the large family of beings known as sasquatch, yeti, yeren, and swamp apes are, in fact, sharing the planet with its other species of beings. These beings have been there for a very long time and have chosen to live in seclusion. Their frightening appearance is intentional, as it aids in maintaining only minimal contact with humans. It is only humans that present any threat to these beings and they are extremely clever about reducing contact. Their habitats are actually quite extensive, but also quite secluded. They live in harmony with their environments and have no need of human contact. Their form bears no resemblance to their intelligence and they are very highly developed beings. They live in strong family units and are very peaceful among themselves. I am sure that you can understand why they hide from humans. They could easily co-exist with humans, but the opposite may not be true. They do have occasional contact with humans, but I believe that it would be very difficult to find an instance where they caused harm to a human. They are aware of the possibility that humans could cause harm to them. In many places where they live, humans have caused great harm to other species with which they once lived, such as bison and wolves. Their caution is not unfounded.

Even as we speak, humans seek them out and are unsatisfied with photographic, visual, and track evidence. They do not desire to be captured or killed so that they might be studied. They will remain elusive until this purpose is removed. These are very adaptable and social creatures, but they do not desire contact with humans. They do not wish to have their remains desecrated out of curiosity and so, upon their passing, their family or clan members dispose of their bodies in a manner that keeps them hidden.

They are not dangerous to humans, but they will frighten them in self defense. It works well. They only wish to be left alone, and so they shall be until they and their families are safe in any dealings with humans. In times long past, ancient humans lived much as these beings lived. Humans sought change. They did not. They are wise of the ways of the plant and animal kingdoms and live in peace with their world and their own kind.

There are many such beings, animals, and plants residing upon the earth that choose to remain hidden by selecting remote locations out of the paths of men. These beings hold much in the way of healing properties and ancient knowledge that will be of benefit in the new earth. When sufficient changes have been settled into the planet's new environment to assure the honor and respect to which they are naturally entitled, these beings shall emerge from hiding and reconnect and rejoin the new earth community. Until such time, they shall remain safely hidden. The new earth shall be a place of respect and trust and it has been the lack of trust and respect that has kept these beings hidden.

Isahal, November 19, 2012

UFO's

I am here. I am your friend Rashka. I am glad that you are taking the time to communicate with us this day. We are always pleased to be in your presence.

Let us talk of the UFOs that are such a topic of interest of late. This interest is no accident. It is both due to an increase in visitations and an increase in information flowing to the earth as a part of the changes underway at this time.

There have always been visitations to that planet from the star seed civilizations. As you and others have suspected, many such visitations became a part of the mythology of ancient civilizations. Many were also documented in the written histories and within the artistic media at the time, but were often misunderstood as time passed, mainly because of the failings of the spoken or written word. It can be difficult at best to describe concepts, events, or phenomena for which the language in use at the time does not contain words to describe what was seen or experienced.

It is inherent in any language form that words are created or invented after they are needed, and not before. So it was always the case that no words had yet been invented to describe the technologies or the life forms encountered. This, of course, left the humans only the option of describing these visitations as closely as possible with the existing language. Is it not true that any species or category of animal or plant form is given a name only after it has been found? Yet, it existed prior to its discovery. And so it was with the visitors and their technology. This is why they were described as wheels of fire, flying chariots, or gods. No other description existed that could explain the unexplainable.

In the times most recently past, there existed a basis for describing the visitors that had been passed down through history and over time much of the awe and fear of these visitations had subsided, because of repeated exposure to these events. A set of forms or models had come to be established for the visitors that had become commonplace enough to cause lessened levels of fear and concern, so the visitors began to manifest in accordance with these models when, in fact, none of these forms are natural forms for the visitors. These models were used simply because they came to conform to the human expectation of an extraterrestrial visitor.

At the same time, many visitations were being made that went unseen because the visitors, being able to manifest in any form that suited them, chose to mimic an existing human or nonhuman form. Still, many chose to resemble the expected form of an alien visitor in an alien craft merely to acclimate humans to the possibility of such visitations. Do you understand? They could have remained disguised or hidden and had no need of a spacecraft, but chose to be seen in what had, by this time, become a nonthreatening manner. This was done to teach humans that there were other beings in the universe; to help in expanding their understanding of the nature of the physical universe in which they live.

Long and longer ago, there were visitations from others whose intent was other than to teach or assist. These beings also chose to play within the limited physical planes, but it came to pass that their influences upon the life forms of the earth were detrimental, and permission for these visitations was withdrawn. This remains in force to this day. No interference of this kind will be allowed by All That Is, as it was not in the best interest of all souls involved and that runs contrary to universal law.

As the new energies are activated, the truth of these visitors will be revealed. This revelation shall be a source of comfort and not a source of fear. Watch for the signs. Prior to the truth of the visitors being revealed, the truth of the fearful acts performed by very human beings and organizations that have been blamed on the visitors will be exposed. After the truth of these acts is understood, it will be safe for the visitors to reveal themselves, in their true forms, without inciting alarm.

Because of the artificial laws of matter and energy placed within the physical planes, humans, lacking knowledge of the true nature of these things, have carried the assumption that these physical laws are universal. Therefore, it is difficult to understand how other civilizations could transcend the obstacles of time and space to visit the earth, and these assumptions have fueled skepticism regarding visitations. It is actually quite comical, and we love to laugh, that humans argue about fuel sources and materials used in alien craft when the craft themselves are completely unnecessary, but are only an illusion created for the benefit of humans. They listen intently for mechanical sounds from beyond the earth's system, while in the vast majority of the created universe mechanical objects are, in fact, an alien concept. Humans are so very creative.

Let us speak again soon, beloved.

Rashka, November 17, 2011

Universal Law of Unity

I am here. I am your friend and teacher. I am called by the name of Isahal. I am glad to be speaking with you again. We have much to discuss this day. May we begin?

Let us speak of the workings of the universal laws. This should be of interest because they will soon once again be applied within the physical planes as the illusion placed upon these planes begins to lift. Please know that the physical laws that have governed places such as the earth system were instituted with intent to assist in maintaining the very physical and material nature of those places. Please know that the material natures of those places were an essential part of the experiment, or game if you prefer, wherein souls could experience a state of less than wholeness for the purpose of learning and experience.

All That Is participated in the creation of these physical planes for the purpose of experiencing the effects of these environments upon the chosen souls who would journey to and through these planes. It is a law of the universe that all is one. All is inseparable and unified in purpose and form. These physical and material planes were created from within the wholeness and unity of All That Is for the express purpose of experiencing a state of less than wholeness, less than perfection, and less than unification.

Please know that there are many versions or models of physical and material planes *and* that each serves the same or similar learning and experiential purposes. Thus, the design and physical workings of each varies slightly from the other, to allow varying levels of limitation upon the souls who play there. By design, some of these physical planes contain more physical diversity among the physical kingdoms present within them. Some contain more light, while some are much darker. The amount of light available was designed to provide varying degrees of difficulty in search of a return to the light.

Because souls that choose to play in these physical dimensions are not limited to only one type of physical environment, many live temporary existences, which you call lifetimes, in other types of physical planes. Often their memory of one plane is carried into another and can be the basis for mythologies that may seen magical or out of place in that plane. Mankind's inventions of mythical places, such as Camelot or Hades for example, are not, in fact, constructs of imagination. They are, instead, memories of other physical planes that contained more light or more darkness than the earth plane, and it is the memories of these very real, albeit very exaggerated, memories, in some circumstances, that fuel the popularity of these myths.

It is also true that some of the ideologies that are believed to have been invented by mankind are also based in memories of other physical planes. Dogmas that have been experimented with in that plane, such as utopian societies and societies based in racial purity, find their foundations in other planes that contain less free will or less diversity among their inhabitants. In these cases of transferred memories of other physical planes, the adherents of these philosophies hold a very firm belief in the correctness of their beliefs, because they carried into that place very strong memories of these other worlds. Most of the core of magical sounding religious histories have been transferred to that place in the memories of souls and have found followers among those who also carry memories of the same worlds on which they were experienced.

Those on earth who would be called zealots are simply those with a stronger attachment to a different physical world than the one in which they currently dwell. The same theory could be applied to those souls who seem to be outside of their preferred time, or those who feel alien to the nature of their biology. They also are more strongly attached to another physical plane. Many with these strong attachments, rather than adapting or adjusting to the earth plane, continue to cross to the plane of their memories for comfort and a sense of belonging. Many of these souls who would seem to be lost in the wrong dimension have incarnated on earth specifically to learn to make these adjustments and to soften their attachments to the other planes. Some will be successful in this, others will not. As you know, neither outcome is wrong. It really is just an experiment in how a soul chooses to experience itself while in a state of less than unity.

Returning to the beginning, I remind you that the universe, being All That Is, is unified in purpose and form. Because of its unity, wholeness, and state of perfection, it cooperated fully in the creation of states of being that were less than whole, less than unified, and less than perfect so that the experience of these artificial states could add to its knowledge of oneness through separateness, knowing all the while that no illusion could harm the perfection of the universe as a whole. No part of All That Is can ever truly be separate. Unity is a law of the universe. The illusion of separation is only maintained within planes or dimensions that are themselves illusions.

I am glad to be of service. Please let us speak again. There is much more that I would be pleased to help you remember.

Isahal, October 30, 2011

Chapter Eight

WORDS OF LOVE

I am here. I am always glad to speak with you. Let us speak of the universal laws, as they are of interest to you. We have spoken in the past of the universal law of unity. This day let us speak of the universal law of love.

All That Is is based in love. We understand that this concept is contrary to the teachings of that world. It is the teachings that are questionable as they relate to love and the creator. The love, of which all the universes are composed, is unconditional love that is pure in form and intent. Any expression or form of love that carries conditions, judgments, or is less than accepting, comforting, and without condition, is incomplete. Rarely, in a physical plane such as yours, is love of universal strength and truth found. Love, in the physical planes, exists, as much else that exists in those places, as only a part of its wholeness. Those planes have not been home to complete and unified manifestations of any nature for a time so long that it cannot be recalled.

At the time of the creation of the universe in which the earth resides, the energies of love were complete. The planet was a paradise of love and unity and all that composed the planet, as well as all that inhabited the planet, thrived in harmony.

There came to be, after a very long time of peace and prosperity upon the planet and within its universe, that a need arose for a sanctuary for souls. That place was not chosen; she volunteered her service. In order for the conditions upon the planet to suit their new purpose as a place of healing, it was necessary to alter her very nature and structure to accommodate these damaged souls. Because these souls had left a part of themselves elsewhere, they required a place in which limitations of the wholeness of creation could be instituted, as their vibration was not harmonious with unity. The vibration of the planet, as it existed, was not consistent with the vibration of the lost souls. That is not the proper term; no soul is ever lost.

In order to allow for a more consistent level of vibration to be reached, changes were made to that universe that, in effect, withdrew or separated enough of the light and love to lower the vibrations to a rate that better suited the souls in need. Because it is not truly possible to separate any part of the whole from itself, instead a veil or curtain, of sorts, was placed that limited or blocked part of the energies from detection. Therefore, from that time forward, the light within the physical universe was not pure and whole and came to be perceived as darker.

The love, which is the energy of all of existence, was perceived as divided. It is not so, but the illusion was masterfully created and the love seemed lessened, elusive, and judgmental. Much as a prism seems to divide light into separate bands of color, these limitations seemed to divide love into a range of emotions of varying vibrations.

Upon the acceptance of her service, the earth and her universe adjusted the thickness and the function of this veil as necessary, for the benefit of her new inhabitants. She has continued this process throughout the eons of time since, as necessary, to maintain vibratory alignments through periods of healing, growth, and recession of her human charges. Her service is great because her love is great.

After a time, as the damaged souls began, under her protection, to heal; the veils were decreased and the planet began to become lighter once again. But, many of the souls who had found respite in her care, as well as many others, decided that there could still be purpose, within the limitations of a physical universe, for growth and learning under a mantle of illusionary separateness. And so it came to be that her service was once again requested and willingly granted, and the veils were once again strengthened. It has remained thus for a very long time, and many souls have benefited by their journeys into that place.

While she would continue to serve in love, the time now approaches for a lifting of these veils and a return to a purer state of being within that place again, because it has been decided by the souls who love that place, the sentience of your universe, and All That Is that the protections are no longer necessary.

I can sense your confusion with the description of the conditions and limitations as protections. Those who long for home voice frustration with the veiled nature of that place. Please remember that the best interests of all souls, as a part of All That Is, are of utmost importance, always. Many that slumber, and many who now awaken from slumber, have been in need of the respite that the limitations have provided. For this reason, the changes that return that place to a higher vibration have been gradual and gentle, so that none are damaged in the process. It could be no other way. Remember that pure love is all-encompassing and cannot, by its very nature, leave even a single soul behind.

Let us speak again soon. I leave you in love and respect.

Isahal, January 14, 2012

I am here. I am glad to be able to speak with you in this way and it is gracious of your beloveds to assist us with this process. I am very glad to be speaking with you and I am proud that you share what you receive so faithfully. I honor your service, as I know that you honor mine. I am honored that you so freely allow me to choose the nature and direction of our discussion, even while you have questions of your own. Please know that I serve and will gladly also address any questions that you have for me. You need only ask.

Let us talk of one of my favorite lessons, love: sweet love, true love, everlasting love, blind love. It is love that flows to and through all of life. It is love that creates all. It is love that feeds the soul and fills the heart. Love is the goal and the method through which the goal is reached. Love not only binds all of the universes, love is all of the universes. All that exists is made of love, contains love, and exemplifies and teaches love. Love underlies all of creation and also supersedes all that is created.

I know that many seek a path to the divine, regardless of the name by which it is called. Please remember that there is no path, no journey, no course of instruction, *and* no initiation or ritual that leads to the divine. God is in each moment and every place and does not need to be sought or found, because he is not lost or separate. Just as heaven is not a place, but a state of being, the divine is not a goal to be neared, attained, or forfeited. It is love: pure love, true love, love everlasting. When evoked, the divine responds with love. When denied, the divine responds with love.

This lesson is so simple, too simple for that world, perhaps. All that is divine is love. All that is matter is love. All that matters is love. Love is what god is and love is where god lives. Seek not the divine in any place, unless that place helps you feel love. Follow no man's path to god, unless that path fills your heart and soul with love. Ask in love. Receive in love. Be love, live love, share love, and in each act of love, god lives. In each thought of love, god lives. Every moment that you hold love in your heart and in your soul and in your life, you hold the divine.

Simple, my dear one. Bless each moment, hold love forth, and be as one with god.

Yeshua ben Yosef, September 12, 2012

I am here. It is lovely to be speaking with you, dearest. I appreciate each and every opportunity to share knowledge and love with my children. There is much to talk about as the new age dawns and I know that you are a patient listener. Thank you for asking to speak with me. May I choose where to begin?

Very good, then. First and foremost, I wish to express my love for all of my children. All who inhabit the planet are as children to me, regardless of their species or class. Please know that I do my best to provide for each and every living thing that places itself in my care. Please know that it is out of love that I shall always honor the divinity of each being and also shall I honor the choices and desires of each. I have willingly and lovingly accepted the responsibility for maintaining and nurturing the planetary system as a service to those souls who have need of such a place. The children of Gaia number almost beyond counting and each is known to my heart in each and all of their lives with me and at all times in their existence.

I love each no more and no less than another; for love is not divisible into places, parts, or times. All that exists is joined by the energies of love and so I choose first to talk of love. All sentiences and souls who serve do so out of love and within love, because love is their essence and love is their beingness. Any state that would seem to be unlike love in any degree is only an illusion. It is part of my chosen service to maintain a system that is an illusion, but this does not mean that my love is limited or diminished in any way. Because I exist and operate within a state of pure love, the restrictions and limitations of my realm do not apply to me and I am not, therefore, subject to the illusion.

Divine love is whole and complete. My sentience is also whole and complete. I offer my service to my children from this state of complete love and divine love is both eternal and self-sustaining. Some among the human children of the earth express concern for my well being and I gratefully accept this concern as a token of love. Some among my human children exhibit little or no concern for my well being and I know that they love me no less. I know and love the essence of all of my children in each moment, fully. I hold each person, each animal, each plant, each element, each force, and each particle of my realm in love that is pure and all inclusive. It is of no concern to me whether any recognize or acknowledge this love. Love is. Love does not need recognition or acceptance to be.

Thank you for talking with me today, dearest. In love, I leave you for now.

Gaia, December 2, 2012

I am here. I am called Sarassa. I am happy to be speaking with you this day. We have been speaking of love and I too wish to send information on this topic. Angels are the exemplification of love and we know it well. It is our purpose to bring the love of the divine into the world in thought and deed. Existing within the love that is god is our honor and our reward.

Love shines brighter than the brightest star in the heavens. Love sings the most beautiful melodies that can be imagined. Love lives and love breathes throughout all of creation. Love is just and fair. Love is accepting of all forms of life in their truth. Love is carried on the wings of angels wherever it is lacking and begs no praise or reward.

Much is made on the earth of unconditional love and it is sought by those souls who reach for spiritual heights and, yet, even unconditional love is lesser in form than divine love. Perhaps this is only a function of language, but the description of love as being without conditions of judgment implies the existence of conditions that would require an overlooking of those attributes that seem less than perfect. By this definition, it would seem that the attainment of a state of unconditional love in a plane of existence that is conditional would not be possible and there is some truth to this. Unconditional love is not of the earth. Unconditional love would more correctly be called divine love. Divinity can be glimpsed from the earth, but it cannot be held within the structure of the earth, except by the divine. It is too large to be properly conceived by the human mind and too bright to be seen by human eyes.

Yet men strive to find love and this search is worthy of the grand souls who choose to be human. They seek an always greater form of love because their hearts remember the truth of love and this connects them to their own perfection.

The heart has no eyes with which to see the light of love and no hands with which to grasp and hold love. The heart can only feel the joy and the beauty of love and this is appropriate. Love holds no form that can be held and examined. Love is an experience and not a possession. Were it not so, then love could be delivered as a gift to the soul and we of the angelic realm would joyfully deliver love to all of creation, if it could be done.

Men yearn for love because they yearn for home. In their search, they can find reminders of the glory of divine love and they will all return to a state of pure love when the journey of each lifetime is complete. The search for love is an honorable and noble pursuit. Any form of love, however incomplete, is better than the lack of love, although in truth, any lack of love is only a matter of perception. Love is the basis of existence and a true lack of love cannot be where there is life. There is no place or situation without life and, so, there is no place or situation without love. Love can seem to be hidden. Love can seem to be lost. Love can seem to be withheld or undeserved. Things are not always as they seem.

Sarassa, December 3, 2012

I am here, my friend. Thank you for calling upon me as you seek messages of love for my people. As a messenger, this service is an essential part of my being and purpose. I am very glad to be of assistance to you in this working. I often speak the words of god in his stead. Therefore, it is completely fitting that we speak of love because there is truth in the saying that god is love. So, let us speak of love, because in so doing we speak of god.

Love expresses itself in ways beyond counting. Love is the core of all existence and is, therefore, contained in all that exists. Because existence allows for many expressions, conditions, and situations that contain life, so do these many expressions, conditions, and situations contain love. Pure love is divine, as you know, but love also adapts its beingness to the lives in which it is contained and the universes that exist, because love is contained within them.

It is said that god, as the living essence of love, sees all and cares for each of his creatures. It would be truer to say that god, as love, is all of his creatures and all of his creations. Where god is, there also is love. Where love is, there also is god. Within those components of existence that exhibit larger expressions of love, god is felt more strongly and seen more clearly. Within those components of existence that experience lesser amounts of love, god seems to be removed and is not seen as clearly. The presence of love, and therefore the presence of god, does not actually vary between any situations or within any universes. It is only the form of expression of love that varies to suit the environments displayed throughout creation. I will remind you that the expression of love draws god near, for these reasons.

It is in love that god is seen. It is in love that god is felt. If god is sought, look not outside of your own living being, for god lives in all that lives. Love in any form or any measure opens the doorway to god. Remember that god is not found by action, but rather is found by being. God is in the moments of love and the moments of stillness within the soul.

For now, I leave you in love.

Gabriel the Messenger, December 6, 2012

I am here. I am your friend and your brother. I also would like to talk to you of love. It is such an important topic of discussion. I know how important staying inside of love is, but I also know how difficult it can be in a physical plane. Any words that I can add to help sustain love in that place would be my honor to send to you.

It is true, as you have been told, that the vibration of love is the same vibration of the energy of creation. In love, all things are truly possible. Words of love, feelings of love, and loving deeds contain the energies of creativity and manifestation. Words of love draw the speaker into the essence of the divine and feed the soul of both the speaker and the recipient, so too with acts of kindness offered in love to one's self and to another. This is why it feels so wonderful to speak and act from love, because doing so has drawn heaven closer in that moment.

Many teachings from many religions and many masters have been offered as reminders of the importance of love above all else. Love given and love received grant their benefits in equal shares. It is love that sustains the soul and the heart, as the home of love in the body that communicates with the love of which the divine is composed. Any word or gesture that is heartfelt is the expression of the divinity of a soul, whether these heartfelt words or deeds are given to another or given to your own self. Offering love to another is a selfless act. Holding love for self is no different. Self love and self respect are the foundations upon which all interactions and relationships with others are built. "Love thy neighbor as thy self" does not instruct to love another instead of self. Remember that all souls are one. Withholding love from self creates a barrier between the heart and the source.

Please know that teachings that discourage self love cannot be in alignment with the divine, because they exclude one, which creates a situation of less than wholeness. Those who practice, preach, or teach unworthiness or exclusion do so as part of a structure of power and control, and their words are false.

It is the way of mankind to love too little, while there is an infinite amount of love available. Speak of love. Give love. Receive love given. Be love and change the world.

Serrale, December 9, 2012

Chapter Nine

An Introduction to the Sources of Information and Teachings And an Explanation of the Process of Channeling

Throughout this work, my words, questions and thoughts have been italicized for clarity about the source of the words. Although I have attempted to remove my personal thoughts wherever possible, there are times that the information relates directly to a question that I posed or a thought that I held at the time the channeling was received. In those instances, my words or thoughts have been included in italics. A great deal of the information that I have received over the years that I have been channeling was of a personal nature or obtained at the request of others and I have attempted to exclude as much as possible of this information, including it only when I feel that the reader may gain insight on a particular issue by its inclusion.

All of the information included in this work was received by automatic writing. In the beginning I used this method because it was effective and I found that this method resulted in less filtering of the information by my own thought processes. As time passed, I continued to use automatic writing because it allowed me to receive information as it flowed and I could read and digest the information at a later time. This has also allowed the channeled information to be saved in its original form, without reliance upon memory or alteration of the actual words received. I very often find different meanings within the words received when they are read again, and so I consider the transcription of the words exactly as received to be important. I find beauty and power in the words of spirit and have been diligent about not changing them.

At this point, I feel it may be of benefit to include a mention of a couple of points of difficultly inherent to channeled information; time and language. Outside of a physical plane of existence time and space do not exist. All that is, was, or will be, from our perspective, already exists for those outside of the physical. From a perspective of timelessness it appears to be extremely difficult to translate the earthly timing of any event. Often "soon" or "very soon" is as close as we get. Unfortunately, I have discovered that "soon" could mean within a few days of earth time or within a few years of earth time. Also, I have found that any information received about a future event is given as the situation exists at the time the information is received, and is always subject to a change of circumstance or can be affected by the free will of the souls involved.

Outside of the physical planes communication is much more telepathic and does not involve only language, but also emotion. It has been explained to me that the use of language can limit the information received to concepts that have words to describe them. As I understand it, outside of the physical planes, when knowledge or experience is shared the whole of the experience or knowledge passes, not just the words that would describe the experience. At times I sense frustration with the translation of concepts into language and often these concepts are expressed as analogies or parables in an attempt to bridge the language barrier. Much of the information received resides between the lines and may require the use of the reader's feelings, experience and imagination to more fully grasp the meaning of the words received.

Where possible, I will use their own words to introduce you to my beloved Serrale, Josiah, Isahal, Allinnana, Laheenah, Sarassa, Michaline, and Rashka, from whom most of the channels were received. Yeshua ben Yosef needs no introduction, as he is Jesus, son of Joseph. Gaia is Mother Earth. Gabriel the Messenger is also known as Archangel Gabriel. We all have guides and teachers assisting us in our journey. The information included in this work has come from some of mine.

Serrale is my Master Guide. You will notice that he often refers to us as brothers, although in this lifetime I am female. Outside of a physical incarnation gender is a non-issue, although his energy feels decidedly male to me, as does the energy of Josiah. Josiah identifies himself as Josiah the Teacher. Isahal is also a teacher. Allinnana is a teacher associated with nature. Their information is often more technical in nature, as one would expect from a teacher. Laheenah is a keeper of feminine energy. Sarassa is an angel. Michaline is a guide and a member of the family of the Archangel Michael, who was contacted on behalf of a dear friend. My friend Sarah has graciously allowed her personal information to be included in chapter four, as it related to soul groups and families. Rashka carries a predominantly female energy, although I admit that in the beginning I visualized her as male, to which she took no offense. She has incarnated in the past and, therefore, seems to have a more complete understanding of the human condition, which often reflects in the information she sends.

Serrale has always been disincarnate. Each of us has a Master Guide who bears the primary responsibility for us, and Serrale is mine. He has been guiding me through all of this lifetime and many others. I have always been very grateful for his guidance and protection during channeling. It is he who decides when others will or will not be allowed to communicate with me directly and he who delivers messages from loved ones who have passed. He also contacts and communicates with the guides of others who have questions from beyond the veil. He insists that communication between the dimensions is a skill that all souls possess. While I agree completely, I must insert a personal word of caution that no one should open to channeling without the guidance and protection of their guide.

I will let a few of these spirits introduce themselves. First, in his own words, meet Josiah the Teacher:

I am a teacher, one of very many teachers on this side. We are always available to instruct whenever asked, both on this side and in the physical planes. We are each specialized to some degree and ask for the assistance of the other teachers when needed. We also work closely with the master guides and the other guides when we are instructing one in another plane, because a master guide is always involved in all aspects of the work of incarnate souls.

They are also, in a way, our students as they monitor all forms of instruction as well as all healing and any requests for assistance during a lifetime.

You understand that when I refer to a lifetime I am talking about a part of a life of a soul spent in a physical incarnation, as that is the only circumstance in which time would apply. Life is eternal. A lifetime is of a limited duration.

We will be instructing both directly, such as this, or indirectly, by placing information within the experiences a soul will have whenever such information is requested, generally by the individual or on its behalf by its guide, or because it is plotted into the plan of a lifetime when certain points of experience are reached and the information is either needed to progress or is needed to correct a course.

The teachers also learn through the experience of teaching, because contact is made with the student and the teacher learns through the experiences of the student. We need to have knowledge of the student in order to know how best to send the information and thus we also learn what the student has learned.

Next, Isahal introduces himself:

I am here. I am called Isahal. It is good to speak with you again. I am glad to answer your questions. I am also a teacher, as is your friend Josiah. I am glad to be able to share information with you in this way. We who teach are engaged in instruction on this side of the veil for those souls who wish to learn and understand while not physically incarnate, as well as teaching in this manner, and others, with souls who are incarnate. Please understand that we learn as much as we teach through contacts such as these. It is an honor to be trusted with your life experiences, they teach us much. As I have always been a teacher or a student, I have not been born into the physical plane. I am, therefore, as curious about the workings of such places as those who seek knowledge of home.

The following are Laheenah's words of introduction:

I am called Laheenah and I am a representative of the circle of feminine energy keepers…As you are always curious about your friends and their stories and origins, I will be happy to discuss these with you as they relate to my circle of energy workers or, perhaps better said, my circle of companions of the feminine energies. We are a group consisting of many souls who were born within and are attuned with the feminine aspect of the creative energies. While it is very true that the energies of creation are whole and balanced, they also contain, in perfect integration, aspects that could be defined as masculine, feminine, and neuter. Although all exist in cooperation and unity, each of these aspects, much like the different aspects of a personality, have an affinity or a preference for certain of the states and acts of creation and are, of course, free to serve where they are the most happy and fulfilled.

And, finally, Rashka:

I will always answer your questions without exception. I am called Rashka. That is as close as the sound of my name can be said in that place. Yes, it contains the sound of Ra and the sound of Ka, as my people were those who planted the seeds of the Egyptian civilization. Yes, it does signify the interaction of the element of light (Ra) and the element of spirit (Ka). I will gladly help you remember the teachings that were given to those peoples so long ago, as this information will be of benefit to you now.

That being said, I sincerely hope that you will find wisdom and love in the words of the guides and teachings presented. Please use your own discernment and, as with all information that you will read and hear from others, take what you need and leave the rest. I am fully aware that each reader will filter this information through his or her own life experience and belief system, and I offer my sincere respect for both. If you find any information that is offered causes you conflict or discomfort, please know that it is absolutely unintentional on my part.

I hope that you will learn and grow from exposure to my guides and teachers, as I have through the years, but also hope that you will listen to your own heart and soul and trust them over any information presented to you from any sources outside of your own wisdom.

Automatic Writing

I believe that all people are able to channel information, and that many are regularly channeling through meditation, prayer and intuition without referring to this process as channeling. Channeling is merely relaxed listening. Some channels step outside of themselves and allow spirit to speak through them. Some use tools, such as stones, pendulums, tarot cards or letter boards to "tune in" to the thoughts or voices of spirit. Some receive information in the form of visions or dreams. This process can be passive, when the channel simply opens up to whatever information may be forthcoming, or active, when the channel searches for specific information by way of a series of questions or requests for signs, or the process may combine the two forms.

Regardless of the method that you find works best for you, it is imperative that proper precautions be taken prior to opening to channel. All information is not created the same. All spirit that is willing to communicate does not necessarily have the best interests of the channel at heart. Both darkness and light exist in varying degrees in all things of this world and not of this world. I never open to channel without first asking for protection and encircling my workspace with white light and asking for the protection of my own guides and angels. I always light a white candle or two, because white signifies protection and spirit is attracted to candle light.

Channeled information can be received from guides, teachers, ascended masters, members of the angelic realm, and one's own higher self or consciousness. The source of the information is directly related to the nature of the information requested or received. Some spirits serve to teach or guide incarnated humans and may or may not have lived human lives themselves.

Each person can access many guides, teachers, and angels for assistance. Guidance and information more directly related to earthly problems and situations will generally be more relevant from a spirit that has been incarnated on earth. Conversely, universal counsel will generally be more relevant from spirit that may never have been incarnate. Specific technical or creative guidance or information will generally be more relevant from a teacher specializing in the related discipline. Guidance related to a soul's plan and purpose will generally be more relevant from a master guide or an angelic being.

All information and guidance received from these sources will come from love. The great reward of channeling is the feeling of unconditional love received from spirit.

Any guidance or information that does not come from love, such as information that is critical, conditional, or demands action or obedience from the channel is not from your soul group and any communication with spirit of this nature should be immediately halted. Channeling without proper protection and guidance can result in contact with earthbound spirits or dark entities. Always ask for communication only with light beings. Darker spirits cannot interact without permission. Do not unintentionally give this permission by forgetting to establish protection before you channel. Many who channel choose to act as mediums between this world and the next and are willing to communicate with earthbound spirits. This is a noble cause where it is done to aid the lost souls or give comfort to the grieving. It is not for amateurs, and should be undertaken only when the channel has learned to protect himself from the darker energies involved and in cooperation with the channel's own guides and protectors. Earthbound spirits and the spirits of the newly crossed can feel heavier and can carry negative emotions, as these spirits have not yet healed in the light. Spirits that have not crossed into the light, or have just recently crossed, are still very much of the earth and information from them may be unreliable, or worse. As you learn to channel, I recommend that communication with these spirits be done only through your guides, who can communicate with these spirits directly or contact the guides of others, thus protecting you from the darker energies.

Why use automatic writing to channel? Please allow me to share the words of Josiah the Teacher on this subject.

I am here. I have been waiting to hear from you again. I am glad that you took time to listen. Let us speak to some of the mysteries. Much of this you already know, but some you do not. There are mysteries of your world that are of interest and mysteries of the universe also. Some are directly related to each other or, rather, a reflection of each other and some do not directly apply to a physical plane such as yours.

You have been using the writing to remind you that words are part of your purpose; to find words for what is difficult to put into words. It is easier to teach in other ways, by experience, but you can see its limitations.

Words can reach so many more, many who would doubt or fear the experience. The written word can be kept and reread until it is understood. It is also not as solitary an experience when proof lies before you in writing that others have seen or sensed the same experience, as an important dream will have more meaning when it is understood that others have had the same dream. This is the value in writing; to share across time and space; to initiate thoughts and experiences in others. In a nonphysical dimension experience can be gained with the merging of souls. In the physical plane this is far more difficult.

Josiah, July 15, 2001

Your guides and angels are dedicated to your service; to protect you and to guide you on your way. The spiritual teachers love to teach. The healers love to assist with your physical and emotional healing. All spirit will respect your path and your choices along your path. They will always respond to your requests for communication and information and will offer up support, comfort, and love. They will wait patiently to hear from you and relish being in your presence. They will work diligently to ease your journey and will send signs that guide and inform. They will rejoice in your triumphs great and small and send light to your darkest hours. Even if you ignore them, deny them, or do not believe in them, they will stay by you in love at all times.

Learning to channel through automatic writing will require time and practice. In the beginning you may not experience much success, but please be patient with the process.

Spirit vibrates at a much higher rate than physical beings. In order for there to be communication, spirit will need to lower its vibratory rate and the channel will need to raise his vibratory rate. Spirit will need to learn to use your physical body to write and will also have to translate thoughts into language. Communication outside of a physical plane is done much differently and much more effectively. When not incarnate, all communication is telepathic. The information or experience being shared is not relayed from one to another; rather the whole of the information or experience is fully shared, seen, and felt by the other. Much is lost in communication that relies only upon words because there is so much information that is experiential in nature and there are many concepts for which language does not contain the proper words to describe. Please be patient.

Before you channel for the first time, I recommend a purposeful meditation to meet your guide. After this meditation you will be able to call upon your guide by name when you channel. It also affords the opportunity to reacquaint yourself with an old friend and acclimate yourself to the feeling of your guide's energy.

Settle into a comfortable position in a safe, quiet place. Ask for the protection of the light and your guides and angels. Focus on your breathing or on a point of light or color until you are fully relaxed. If you do not have much experience meditating, be patient with yourself. If your mind wanders or you are distracted, simply refocus and try again. When you are relaxed visualize yourself in a safe, beautiful place and ask your guide or your angel to join you. Explain that you will be learning to speak to them in channel and ask for them to meet with you. You may get a mental picture of them or you may just feel their presence when they arrive. Spirit will communicate with you in words, but it may seem more like hearing thoughts than hearing words. Trust what you see and feel. Ask their name. Believe what you hear. Ask why they guide you and they will respond with an expression of love. If they do not, ask that they leave and ask again to meet your guide or angel. Your guide will only come to you in love. Trust what you feel. When you are ready, thank your guide for their presence and their assistance. Thank the light for its protection and you are ready to return.

I also suggest that you ground yourself before you channel. I use a simple grounding ritual whenever I feel that I am disconnected from the physical, which you may find helpful. During times of stress I may use this exercise several times a day.

Take a couple of deep breaths, close your eyes, relax and visualize roots, like the roots of a tree, growing down into the earth from your feet. If you prefer, you can also send a grounding cord down into the earth from your first, or root, chakra. Visualize these roots spreading out and down deep into the center of the earth, connecting your physical being to the physical earth. Ask that your physical energy fields be attuned to the vibrations of the ascending earth. This exercise is helpful whenever your personal energy feels disrupted and it helps your physical body stay nurtured and protected while in channel.

You will only need to enter a light trance state in order to use automatic writing. A light trance is the state reached during meditation and is merely a state of deep relaxation. I will use excerpts from the words of Josiah the Teacher to explain.

I am of your group of instructors and I will, of course, protect as I instruct. This work done in a trance state does, as you suspect, create a sort of vulnerability but you can easily protect yourself. It involves the creation of an altered state of consciousness that allows for a freer flow of information and also loosens some of the physical constraints making it easier to exert your energy upon the physical dimension.

It would be best at first to practice putting yourself into trance states. The one you are experiencing now *(as I was channeling this message)* is a light trance because you are aware of your physical surroundings. This state is easy to access.

The next level of trance is a medium trance. This state has less contact with the physical and is more like a sleeping state. Quiet is best when practicing this state. It will be used for more direct communication between the dimensions and also to tap into your kinetic powers.

The deepest level of trance will always require spirit protection because you will be removed from physical form and will need assistance with your return and maintenance of the validity of the physical environment in your absence. A physical form absent of spirit is very vulnerable.

Josiah, March 15, 1998

In order to practice channeling you will need a safe, comfortable, quiet space. I recommend clearing your workspace often by burning sage or incense and requesting that the area be cleansed of any negative energy. You will also need writing materials, such as a notebook and pencil or pen. Channeling can be very physically tiring. It uses a lot of your energy to alter your vibration. In the beginning I suggest short sessions followed by a period of rest. You will need to be as comfortable as possible in order to meditate with the fewest distractions. Please set aside sufficient time for your practice so that you are not disturbed by time commitments when the information begins to flow. While in channel you will find that you lose your sense of time. Do not be concerned. This is a sign that you are doing it right.

If you share your space with pets, please consider their needs. Animals are extremely sensitive to the energy of spirit. They are naturally adept at balancing the energies of their environments. If you channel powerful spirits, the energetic changes may irritate your animal friends and it is best to remove them from your workspace to avoid disturbing them and distracting you.

Sit comfortably, light a white candle or two. I prefer to channel in dim light or darkness by candlelight. I find it less distracting than a well lighted area. It may not be so for you, so please do what feels best for you. Please turn off sources of noise and, as you are learning, electronics. Many channels use computers and transcribe the information directly into the computer as it is received. You may prefer this method as you become more proficient. I still use pencil and paper. I love the information that I receive and transcribing it at a later time allows me to process the words another time. I often find different shades of meaning in the words when I work with them later. Situate your writing materials. Ask for the protection of the white light as you channel. Call upon your guide or angels and ask what spirit would like you to know. Holding the pen or pencil to the paper lightly, relax and wait for the pencil to move. It may not happen the first time, or the first couple of times, that you try to channel. Be patient. The first time you receive writing it may be difficult or impossible to read. Be patient. This is a learning process for both you and spirit. Each time you try your results will improve. The person who taught me automatic writing was distrustful that she was receiving the information from a source other than her own hand, so she intentionally held the pencil in her non-dominant hand. Feel free to try this.

When your practice session is complete, be sure to thank your guides or angels and thank the light for its protection before extinguishing the candle(s). Please also be sure to close any communication portals that you have opened. An opening between the dimensions can allow passage into the physical world of nonphysical beings and energies. They can be quite annoying. Should you neglect to close a portal, call upon your guide for help in sending the energies back to their dimension and closing the portal behind them.

At first, the information you receive may be illegible or confusing. This will improve with time. You will also learn to trust the process. I too doubted the source of the information that I received when I began, but as I received more and more information that I did not know or remember I stopped doubting.

As I am writing, I can tell when I am receiving the thoughts of others and when I am tapping into my own wisdom. There have been many times that this method of hearing my own wisdom has been very helpful. I have learned to distinguish the cadence of my own thoughts from the thoughts of others. When receiving the words of others, I am often surprised by the words as they flow onto paper.

When reading these channels, I hope that you will see that the style of the writings from different guides and teachers vary. Their energy signatures also vary in intensity. I find that their individual handwriting varies also. I have learned to trust. You will too.

Recommended Reading

Your Soul's Plan, Discovering the Real Meaning of the Life You Planned Before You Were Born, by Robert Schwartz, Frog Books, 2009, originally released under the title *Courageous Souls.*

Your Soul's Gift, The Healing Power of the Life You Planned Before You Were Born, by Robert Schwartz, Whispering Winds Press, 2012.

Robert Schwartz is the definitive authority on pre-birth planning. I highly recommend his books on this subject for further understanding of the pre-birth process and its implications within individual lives. His thorough and sensitive treatment of the subject is both informative and healing.

CPSIA information can be obtained at www.ICGtesting.com
Printed in the USA
BVOW012035300113

312008BV00003B/258/P